Praise For

The Politically Incorrect Guide® to
Economics

"In the spirit of Regnery's Politically Incorrect series, Professor DiLorenzo de-bamboozles economics in the most engaging ways possible. From markets to monopolies, from 'perfect competition' nirvana to socialist predation, this book is maybe the single best introduction (or refresher) to economics I've ever seen. Bravo!"

> —**Jeff Deist**, president of the Ludwig von Mises Institute

"Since its onset during the Progressive Era, the economics profession has been the handmaiden of political power. Thankfully, Thomas DiLorenzo is a card-carrying member of an older, nobler tradition in economics. He has spent his illustrious career speaking truth to power and louder than ever in his latest book, *The Politically Incorrect Guide to Economics.*"

> —**Dr. Jeffrey Herbener**, chair of the Department of
> Economics and Sociology, Grove City College

"In his characteristically lively, engaging style, Tom DiLorenzo knocks down one myth after another about the alleged shortcomings of markets and competition. A great introduction not only to economic policy, but also to how (good) economists think."

> —**Peter Klein**, professor of entrepreneurship at
> Baylor University

"*The Politically Incorrect Guide to Economics* by Thomas DiLorenzo is the *Economics in One Lesson* (by the late, great Henry Hazlitt) for the twenty-first century, a must-read for everyone who values economic freedom over bureaucratic control, political cronyism, and socialism."

> —**David Stockman**, former Michigan congressman and
> director of the U.S. Office of Management and Budget in
> the Reagan administration

The Politically Incorrect Guide® to Economics

Be sure to check out

The Politically Incorrect Guides® to...

American History
Thomas Woods
9780895260475

The American Revolution
Larry Schweikart
Dave Dougherty
9781621576259

The Bible
Robert J. Hutchinson
9781596985209

The British Empire
H. W. Crocker III
9781596986299

Capitalism
Robert P. Murphy
9781596985049

Catholicism
John Zmirak
9781621575863

Christianity
Michael P. Foley
9781621575207

The Civil War
H. W. Crocker III
9781596985490

Communism
Paul Kengor
9781621575870

The Constitution
Kevin R. C. Gutzman
9781596985056

Darwinism and Intelligent Design
Jonathan Wells
9781596980136

English and American Literature
Elizabeth Kantor
9781596980112

The Founding Fathers
Brion McClanahan
9781596980921

Global Warming
Christopher C. Horner
9781596985018

The Great Depression and the New Deal
Robert Murphy
9781596980969

Hunting
Frank Miniter
9781596985216

Immigration
John Zmirak and Al Perrotta
9781621576730

Islam (And the Crusades)
Robert Spencer
9780895260130

Jihad
William Kilpatrick
9781621575771

The Middle East
Martin Sieff
9781596980518

The Presidents, Part 1
Larry Schweikart
9781621575245

The Presidents, Part 2
Steven F. Hayward
9781621575795

Real American Heroes
Brion McClanahan
9781596983205

Science
Tom Bethell
9780895260314

The Sixties
Jonathan Leaf
9781596985728

Socialism
Kevin D. Williamson
9781596986497

The South (And Why It Will Rise Again)
Clint Johnson
9781596985001

The Vietnam War
Phillip Jennings
9781596985674

Western Civilization
Anthony Esolen
9781596980594

Women, Sex, and Feminism
Carrie L. Lukas
9781596980037

The Politically Incorrect Guide® to
Economics

Thomas J. DiLorenzo

Regnery Publishing
WASHINGTON, D.C.

Regnery® is a registered trademark and its colophon is a trademark of Salem Communications Holding Corporation

Cataloging-in-Publication data on file with the Library of Congress

ISBN: 978-1-68451-298-0
eISBN: 978-1-68451-313-0

Published in the United States by
Regnery Publishing
A Division of Salem Media Group
Washington, D.C.
www.Regnery.com

Manufactured in the United States of America

10 9 8 7 6 5 4 3 2 1

Books are available in quantity for promotional or premium use. For information on discounts and terms, please visit our website: www.Regnery.com.

*Dedicated to the memory of my friend and colleague,
Professor Walter E. Williams, champion of freedom and economic
educator extraordinaire*

Contents

Introduction

In the academic world, university economics departments are usually where you will find the most conservatives and the least politically correct foolishness. Understanding even the most elementary economic principles inoculates one against the utopian fantasies of liberals and socialists—such as curing poverty with minimum wage laws (why not make it $1,000 per hour and end poverty once and for all?); controlling inflation with price-control laws (yeah, like Nixon did); enriching the working class by taking more money out of their pockets in taxes; cutting the cost of medical care by giving government bureaucrats a *monopoly* in its provision; putting the nation's entire money supply under the control of political appointees in a secret organization (the Fed) that has never been audited; giving politicians legal rights to counterfeit money ("monetary policy"); and so forth. This is why economists are often treated like the skunks at the picnic by liberal and socialist utopians in academe and elsewhere. They point out the obvious.

This general truth is far from universal, however; there are plenty of economics departments at American universities where just about everyone is to the left of a Hillary Clinton or a Barack Obama. Then there are the

A Book You're Not Supposed to Read

James T. Bennett and Thomas J. DiLorenzo, *Official Lies: How Washington Misleads Us* (Alexandria, Virginia: Groom Publishing, 1993).

Government lies to us about just about everything.

celebrity economists chosen by the government elites and crony capitalist corporate bureaucrats who are featured on the network television stations and in the *New York Times* and the *Washington Post*. Some of them, like Clinton administration labor secretary Robert Reich, are not even economists but lawyers and political hacks.

Most people largely ignore economics because, let's face it, "the dismal science" (Thomas Carlyle's name for it) is not quite as simple and easy as watching a TV sitcom or an episode of *Wheel of Fortune*. Most of what average citizens think they know about the subject comes from brief snippets they see on TV or read in the *Times* or the *Post* by celebrity economists such as Paul Krugman, former officials like Robert Reich, or government bond salesmen from some Wall Street bank or hedge fund.

Much of what such people say about economics is politically correct propaganda and pure hokum. Their job is to create what free-market economist Ludwig von Mises called official myths about economics and government. The job of real economists, said Mises, is to unmask some of these myths. That is exactly what this book proposes to do.

Internationally known investor and author Doug Casey forcefully explained how this all works in an essay with the catchy title of "How Economic Witch Doctors Convince Everyone They're Neurosurgeons." Most economists, writes Casey, "are political apologists masquerading as economists." They "prescribe the way they would like the world to work and tailor theories to help politicians demonstrate the virtue and necessity of their quest for more power."

The field of economics "has been turned into the handmaiden of government in order to give a scientistic justification for things the government…wants to do." The antidote to this, says Casey, is not to spend hundreds of thousands of dollars on a college degree in economics but to educate yourself. "[E]very person should be his own economist" after undergoing such self-education, he says, repeating the advice of twentieth-century free-market economist Ludwig von Mises.[1]

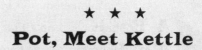

★ ★ ★

Pot, Meet Kettle

Doug Casey says that economists "have become an excuse for central planning,"[2] and he is right. And to think that we used to criticize the Soviets for centrally planning *their* economy.

Given this state of affairs, the main purpose of this book is twofold: first, to explain and criticize many of the false theories that have evolved primarily to prop up government power and enrich the ruling class, not to improve the economy; and second, to help you, the reader, to become your own economist—and hence a better citizen.

The Remnant

There has always been a remnant of economic educators who understood and taught their students about the value of private property, free markets, free trade, and economic freedom—along with the perils and inevitable failures of government interventionism. This "remnant" consists of three basic schools of economic thought whose ideas will be discussed throughout this book: 1) the Austrian School of economics, so named because its founders were from Austria, the best known of whom is the Nobel laureate F. A. Hayek; 2) the Chicago School of free-market economics most associated with another Nobel laureate, Milton Friedman; 3) and the Public Choice School, associated with your author's graduate school professor and onetime colleague, Nobel laureate James M. Buchanan. This last school of thought, which uses economic theory and methodology to analyze government behavior, is known for its theory of "government failure."

In today's crazed world of academic "wokeness," the new word for political correctness, it is not uncommon for professors who espouse such views to be libeled, slandered, and even chased off campus. Exhibit A is the experience of the college campus speakers' series administered by the conservative organization Young America's Foundation, whose speakers have been shouted down, canceled, harassed, disinvited, and threatened. Some universities have even demanded that they spend tens of thousands of dollars for extra "security" should they sponsor a campus lecture by a—horrors!—conservative speaker.

Anything that challenges the politically correct orthodoxy—in economics, and virtually all other fields—is likely attacked by the campus Left, sometimes violently. When yours truly was invited to give a lecture in defense of capitalism and economic freedom at a North Carolina college, I discovered that extra campus police and security guards had been called in, apparently just in case anything was said that the campus Marxists found to be insensitive!

The Socialist Founders of the American Economic Association

Economics as a profession was founded in 1885 by late nineteenth-century versions of today's politically correct professors. The leaders of the movement were men like Richard T. Ely. Ely was an American who had gone to Germany to pursue graduate studies at a time when German academe had decided to abandon virtually all of the economic theory that had been developed up to that time, from Adam Smith, author of the most famous treatise in economics, *The Wealth of Nations*, to their own time. In its place they had put a method of studying and researching "economics" that involved using statistics and historical facts in an ad hoc way to essentially crusade for a welfare state, government regulation of business, and socialism. It was called the German Historical School.

So members of the new American Economic Association decided to disavow the traditional methods and theories of economics in order to create a false façade of "science" for their socialistic political preferences. They were well aware that economic logic and common sense invalidated many of their utopian government interventions, so they opted to ignore economic logic and common sense.

★ ★ ★

Lying with Statistics

"There are three kinds of lies: lies, damned lies, and statistics," according to Mark Twain, who attributed the saying to Disraeli. "If you torture the data long enough, it will confess" seems to have been the unofficial motto of the German Historical School economists.

The founding document of the American Economic Association (AEA) threw down the gauntlet to the other economic scholars at the time (the Remnant) who still valued the previous century or more of economic scholarship. That document praised the state as "an educational and ethical agency whose positive aid is an indispensable condition of human progress" while condemning "the doctrine of laissez-faire" (a.k.a. economic liberty) as "unsafe in politics and unsound in morals." The document also included some Marxist class-conflict language, declaring, "We hold that the conflict of labor and capital has brought to the front a vast number of social problems whose solution is impossible without the united efforts of Church, state, and science."[3]

By "science" the founders of the American Economic Association apparently meant their own personal opinions and policy preferences, expressed in academic jargon and made almost impossible for the average person to understand, to be imposed on the public by the state with the blessings of the "Church."

> ★ ★ ★
>
> ## No Wall of Separation
>
> Unlike today's "progressives," the original "progressives" such as Ely and his comrades had no problem with the *non*-separation of church and state. Many of them were "pietists" who believed a collaboration of church and state, under their supervision, could and should stamp out "sin" and create a version of heaven on earth.[4]

The AEA's declaration-of-purpose document was eventually changed because so many in the new profession of academic economics had studied, well, economics, and not just the manipulation of statistics to "justify" statism, interventionism, and socialism. That backtracking returned the field to the arena of healthy intellectual debate, but not for long.

The Great Depression was a turning point when academic economists realized for the first time that they didn't have to spend their work lives in stuffy college classrooms but could become directors of government agencies and advisors to presidents. And at higher pay to boot! It doesn't take a genius to realize that the kind of advice that would be wanted would be to give more power, money, and influence to the government to "manage" the economy, just as Doug Casey points out.

The so-called Keynesian Revolution was revolutionary because the 1936 book by British economist John Maynard Keynes, titled *The General Theory of Employment, Interest, and Money*, seemed to provide an intellectual rationale for an American version of central planning through monetary and fiscal (taxing and spending) policy. It was the perfect "scientistic" smokescreen for increased governmental power, as Doug Casey would say. Keynesianism swept the economics profession, while at the same time there was a proliferation of stylized theories of "market failure" blaming the Great Depression—and virtually all other economic ailments—on too much economic freedom, too much prosperity, and not enough government supervision, bureaucracy, and central planning. Many of these theories will be discussed—and dissected—in detail in the chapters of this book.

By the end of World War II the economics profession had become dominated by interventionists of all kinds, including socialists, and it would remain so for the next several decades. Things seemed bleak for the relatively small number of old-school free-market economists who, led by F. A. Hayek, established the Mont Pelerin Society in 1947. The society was named after a mountain in the Alps where this remnant of academic defenders of freedom held their first meeting to discuss how to oppose the burgeoning trend towards socialism throughout the world. Hayek, Milton Friedman, Henry Hazlitt, Karl Popper, Leonard Read, and Ludwig von

A Book You're Not Supposed to Read

Henry Hazlitt, *The Failure of the New Economics: An Analysis of the Keynesian Fallacies* (Eastford, Connectict: Martino Fine Books, 2016).

Hazlitt's complete refutation of Keynes's General Theory was originally published in 1959. History proves that Hazlitt was right on the money and Keynes was dead wrong.

Mises were among the best-known conservative and libertarian scholars who attended that first meeting. Ludwig Erhard, chancellor of Germany from 1966 to 1969, was also a prominent member of the Mont Pelerin Society. As the German minister of economic affairs under the occupation authorities, he deregulated the German economy after the war on a single day in 1948, igniting the "German economic miracle."[5]

By the 1970s the Keynesian-interventionist-socialist dominance of economics began to crumble thanks to "stagflation"—higher unemployment and inflation at the same time—created by all the government intervention. The Keynesians had no explanation for stagflation; in fact, one of their core principles was that inflation and unemployment are always *inversely* related. There was a resulting resurgence of free-market economics, with Hayek being awarded the Nobel Prize in economics in 1974 and Friedman in 1976. The Keynesian era seemed to have run its course, and the Chicago, Austrian, and Public Choice schools were gaining ground—and adherents. Theirs were the economic ideas that were embraced by the Reagan and

> ★ ★ ★
> ## Pledging Her Faith
> British prime minister Thatcher is said to have stormed into a cabinet meeting, slammed one of Hayek's books onto a table, and said, "*This* is what we believe in!"

Thatcher administrations of the late 1970s and early 1980s.

The point of this brief sketch of some aspects of the history of the American economics profession is that "liberal" or leftist ideas have indeed dominated economics for long periods of history, but there has always been a remnant of influential economic thinkers who, although outnumbered in academe, have been very effective communicators of economic ideas—politically incorrect ideas.

A sampling of these ideas, taken from the vast literature of economics from the past several decades, thoroughly footnoted and written in plain English, is what this book is all about. Among the politically incorrect ideas you will encounter are: why markets work but governments do not; why political control of prices is the worst economic idea in history; how liberal economists make careers out of attacking phony, straw-man arguments; why capitalism is the cure for, not the cause of, most environmental problems; why almost everything you may have learned in college (or elsewhere) about "market failure" is false; why failure is "success" in government; why regulation is always the *cause* of monopoly, not the solution; the anatomy of the government's job-destroying and boom-and-bust-creating machinery; why "trade agreements" are anti–free trade; the Fed's hundred-year record of failure; the economic poison of socialism; and more. Along the way, you will be introduced to dozens of books the left-liberal establishment doesn't want you to read—which means of course you certainly should! Reading this book will put you well on the road to becoming your own economist.

Thomas J. DiLorenzo
Bluffton, South Carolina
March 2022

CHAPTER 1

What Is "the Free Market," Anyway?

No institution in the world does a better job of encouraging human cooperation for the benefit of society as a whole than the much-denigrated free-market economy. Human beings long ago figured out that they all had a much better chance of surviving and prospering if they could rely on what economists call "the division of labor." Just imagine what it would be like if you had to grow your own food; raise or capture and kill your own chickens, cows, hogs, and other animals for meat; make you own bread; build your own house; manufacture your own vehicles; and do everything else for yourself. We would all still be living like cavemen and cavewomen, not even rising to the level of Fred and Wilma Flintstone.

The free market is an institution in which people *specialize* in myriad different tasks that they accumulate experience and expertise in doing. Whether a person's skill involves working alone or as part of a team or group, whether in a small business or a large corporation, if that skill is valued by others, then he will be remunerated for his efforts with money. He will then use that money to buy *his* necessities of life (and fun and leisure products and services as well), produced by people with skills at performing thousands of *other* tasks. That's how the division of labor works. It is also why,

A Book You're Not Supposed to Read

Henry Hazlitt, *Economics in One Lesson* (Auburn, Alabama: Mises Institute, 2020).

The best introductory economics book ever written.

in a free-market economy, even the poorest people can live a decent life—with prospects of rapid improvement, thanks to economic freedom—because they do not have to rely on their own efforts alone. They can find inexpensive food, clothing, housing, and essentially all other necessities of life, provided by entrepreneurs who themselves prosper by serving them.

To give just one example, the late Sam Walton, the founder of Walmart, became one of the wealthiest men in the world by figuring out how to cut the price of just about everything to the benefit of everyone, but especially of lower-income consumers. That's one of the other virtues of the free market: it rewards people who can figure out how to supply products and services that might have originally only been affordable to the wealthy so cheaply that just about anyone can afford and enjoy them. Henry Ford became wealthy by producing cheaper and cheaper (and better and better quality) automobiles; John D. Rockefeller became wealthy by selling refined kerosene and other oil industry products cheaper and cheaper for decades; Cornelius Vanderbilt got his start in business by managing a steamship business on the Hudson River in which the ride was *free* (!), making money by selling food and drinks on board; and on and on.[1] For their efforts such men have been denigrated by the enemies of economic freedom (including various politicians, government bureaucrats, socialist ideologues in academe, journalism, and elsewhere) as "robber barons." Of course, they did not "rob" anyone. Unlike government, they could not *force* anyone to buy their products; they had to *persuade* people to buy them by making them cheaper and better.

Only government can *rob* you of your hard-earned money by threatening imprisonment for refusal to pay what it demands of you for services or products that you may have no need for whatsoever, and whose existence you may even deeply resent. It's called tax evasion, a crime that is punished under federal and state law by fines, imprisonment, or both. That is why the most menial local government tax-collecting bureaucrat can have more power over your life than the wealthiest businessperson in the world. Businesspeople must *persuade* people to purchase more of their products or services; unelected government bureaucrats can *order* you to shut down your business, take your kids

out of school, or quit your job, and get the police to enforce the orders (as all Americans learned during the pandemic of 2020–2022).

Consider, for a moment, the fact that it would be humanly impossible for you and any twenty or so of your friends and acquaintances to make a simple pizza *from scratch*. What ingredients would you need? Well, first of all there's the crust. Therefore, you would need a wheat field to grow the wheat that can be turned into flour for the crust—and all the technology that goes into manufacturing the tractors and other farm machinery that are necessities to a wheat farmer. You would also need oil wells and oil refineries to refine the oil into gasoline or diesel fuel for the tractors, trucks, and other vehicles, along with all the technical engineering knowledge required for such an endeavor. Not to mention the creation of capital markets to arrange financing for such a large undertaking.

Then there's the flour mill, and all the technology involved in turning wheat into flour and, once again, the transportation resources and technology required to deliver the flour to market. There are the tomatoes for the sauce and the tomato farm; the dairy farm to generate the cheese for your pizza; and the vegetables, sausage, and so forth.

★ ★ ★

Not So Darwinian

The division of labor destroys the hoary myth that the free market is a matter of the "survival of the fittest." Even the most unfit can live a decent life while striving to ascend to a "fitter" or even the "fittest" category through education, training, on-the-job experience, entrepreneurship, and perseverance. That is why migration of the world's poor is always in the direction of countries where there is more economic freedom (a synonym for "the free market") and away from countries where there is less.

So, as you can see, it would be impossible and unthinkable for a family or even the residents of a small city to make a pizza from scratch without the benefits of the division of labor—let alone something more complicated, like an automobile or a computer. The division of labor in a free society where people are free to pursue making money through their own hard work is the glue that holds human civilization together.

The eighteenth-century Scottish moral philosopher Adam Smith authored what is arguably the most famous single paragraph ever in economic literature in his 1776 book *An Inquiry into the Nature and Causes of the Wealth of Nations* (usually referred to as just *The Wealth of Nations*). At the time (the year of the Declaration of Independence, by the way), Europe was being transformed from a system of feudalism to a more-or-less free-market economy with the advent and invention of capitalist institutions.

There was much interest in Adam Smith's day in whether or not this apparently self-interested pursuit of money was good or bad for the average person in European society. Smith concluded yes, it *was* good for society because of the division of labor—and because of what came to be known as "the invisible hand." As Smith wrote,

> In civilized society [man] stands at all times in need of the cooperation and assistance of great multitudes, while his whole life is scarce sufficient to gain the friendship of a few persons.... Man has almost constant occasion for the help of his brethren, and it

is in vain for him to expect it from their benevolence only. He will be more likely to prevail if he can interest their self-love in his favour, and show them that it is for their own advantage to do for him what he requires of them. Whoever offers to another a bargain of any kind proposes to do this: Give me that which I want, and you shall have this which you want, is the meaning of every such offer; and it is in this manner that we obtain from one another the far greater part of those good offices which we stand in need of. *It is not from the benevolence of the butcher, brewer, or the baker, that we expect our dinner, but from their regard to their own interest.* Nobody but a beggar chuses to depend chiefly upon the benevolence of his fellow citizens. [Emphasis added.][2]

A Book You're Not Supposed to Read

Nathan Rosenberg and Richard Birdsall, *How the West Grew Rich* (New York: Basic Books, 1984).

How property rights and economic freedom made the West more prosperous and free than anywhere else on earth.

The words in italics comprise the famous "invisible hand theorem." The point is not that the pursuit of "self-love" or self-interest is *always* a good thing, only that a person's desire to support himself and his family through commerce or the free market can only be successful if he offers his fellow man something that he wants and values: *Give me that which I want (money), and you shall have this which you want (a valued product or service).* Free-market exchange or trade is always mutually beneficial; otherwise it would not take place. In the language of game theory, voluntary free-market exchange is a "positive-sum game" that benefits both buyer and seller. Competition in the marketplace harnesses the natural human proclivity for self-preservation in a way that benefits the entire society. From a moral perspective, Rabbi Daniel Lapin makes a telling point in discussing

A Book You're Not Supposed to Read

Thomas Sowell, *Basic Economics* (New York: Basic Books, 2014).

By one of the most brilliant economists of our time—or any time.

this topic when he says that he would "not be surprised" to learn some day that God approves of a system in which everyone prospers by serving his fellow human beings either as a buyer or seller.[3] Adam Smith, like Rabbi Lapin, was a moral philosopher who studied economics as well. He would likely agree.

Entrepreneurship: Economic and Political

Most people seem to equate "business" and "commerce" with big business—the automobile industry, the insurance companies, the giant media corporations, the computer industry, etc. It all seems so complex to the ordinary citizen, but the fundamental economic principle of the benefit of the free market under the division of labor can perhaps be understood better on a smaller scale. A good set of examples is from the enormously popular television program *Shark Tank*, where entrepreneurs with business ideas, new products or services, or both make a pitch to several wealthy investors they want to invest in their new business or business idea. As of this writing the most successful *Shark Tank* products, each of which went from nothing to sales of over $100 million in just a year or two, included heat-free hair rollers for women, eco-friendly flower deliveries, blankets with hoods for those cold winter nights up North, a stylized toilet seat, a sponge with a smiley face that hardens in cold water and softens in warm water, and a socks-and-T-shirt business that donates a product to homeless charities for each one sold.[4]

In each case an entrepreneur asked the question: What problem can I help my fellow citizens solve with a product or service? There are, of course, many products and services that don't solve other people's problems very well, but the above-mentioned products and services have, as measured by their enormous popularity—and profits.

Speaking of products that don't sell, in the free market even business *failures* have a value: people are not omniscient, and business failures at least tell us what people *don't* want despite the best efforts of hopeful entrepreneurs. One thing the free market has going for it in this regard is that the entrepreneurs who create such products and services have a personal financial stake in them. This doesn't guarantee success, but it creates the right incentive. There is a free-market feedback mechanism whereby products and services that please consumers are rewarded with profits, whereas products and services that do not please consumers are punished with losses and bankruptcies.

With government (the only other means besides the free market of allocating resources in society), by contrast, no politician or government bureaucrat ever has a red cent of his or her own money invested. When their services and programs fail miserably, as they often do, they usually respond by doubling down or tripling down with even more tax dollars—just the opposite of the losses or bankruptcies that follow failed private businesses. In government, failure to serve the public is "success" from a financial perspective. If your government job is to reduce poverty but poverty increases instead, you get a *bigger* budget. If your government job is to educate children but test scores keep getting worse and worse, your school system will get a bigger and *bigger* budget. Government entities always and everywhere proclaim that the only reason they have failed at their mission is that they weren't given enough taxpayer dollars. How ironic that government bureaucrats routinely call themselves "public *servants.*"

The pursuit of self-interest in politics and government is almost *never* to the benefit of everyone involved. By definition, a majority-rule democracy is always a matter of a majority imposing its will on an electoral minority, using the coercive powers of the state to force or compel that minority to

> ★ ★ ★
> ## Who's for Dinner?
> Benjamin Franklin is said to have defined democracy as two wolves and a lamb voting on what to have for dinner. All three animals get to vote, but the outcome is not likely to be beneficial to all three.

pay for government programs that it voted against and does not want. It is not voluntary and mutually beneficial any more than an armed robbery on a city street corner is. The politicians themselves prosper in their careers, and various special-interest groups that comprise the majority are satisfied, but it all comes at the expense of the minority. At best, politics is a zero-sum game where one group's benefits come at the expense of costs imposed upon another group or groups. It has been many generations since the federal government stuck to its legal and constitutional duties as outlined in Article 1, Section 8, of the Constitution: national defense, maintaining the federal judiciary, enforcing patents, regulating foreign trade, establishing citizenship, and the like—things that one could argue *do* benefit just about everyone by creating a stable society.[5] Those things have become smaller and smaller percentages of all federal spending over the years, as government has become essentially the auctioneer of a gigantic transfer society, "buying" votes with taxpayer dollars by imposing taxes on one segment of society in order to subsidize political supporters in a larger segment. Unlike the free market, politics is *inherently conflictual*.

The Consumer Is King

Unless they are granted special government favors or subsidies, big businesses in a free market can only become "big" by pleasing large numbers of customers, period. In that sense they are not different from the *Shark Tank* entrepreneurs. Indeed, most of them started out as small businesses or even sole proprietorships. Walmart founder Sam Walton started out with a single small grocery store with a $20,000 investment from his father-in-law. The

Microsoft Corporation started out in Bill Gates's father's garage in Palo Alto, California. John D. Rockefeller saved every penny in his early life from various jobs until he could buy a single oil refinery in Cleveland for $24,000, which eventually became the Standard Oil Company.

Economist Ludwig von Mises, a refugee from Nazi Germany and the preeminent intellectual critic of socialism during the twentieth century,[6] explained the imperative to serve consumers that is the cornerstone of any free-market economy:

A Book You're Not Supposed to Read

Thomas DiLorenzo, *How Capitalism Saved America: The Untold History of Our Country, from the Pilgrims to the Present* (New York: Three Rivers Press/Random House, 2004).

How free-market entrepreneurship produces freedom and prosperity, and how government intervention destroys it.

> Neither the entrepreneurs nor the farmers nor the capitalists determine what has to be produced. The consumers do that. If a businessman does not strictly obey the orders of the public as they are conveyed to him by the structure of market prices, he suffers losses, he goes bankrupt.... Other men who did better in satisfying the demand of the consumers replace him.... The consumers...make poor people rich and rich people poor. They determine precisely what should be produced, in what quantity, and in what qualities. They are merciless egoistic bosses, full of whims and fancies, changeable and unpredictable.... They do not care a whit for past merit and vested interests.... In their capacities as buyers and consumers they are hard hearted and callous, without consideration for other people.[7]

In other words, it is businesses in a free market who are the *real* "public servants." Moreover, the free market is neutral, in the sense that it works to give the consumers what they want. If you are unhappy that your fellow

A Book You're Not Supposed to Read

Ludwig von Mises, *Human Action* (Auburn, Alabama: Mises Institute, 2001).

The great treatise of the twentieth century's preeminent scholar of capitalism and critic of socialism.

citizens spend too much of their money on booze and not enough on Bibles, that is not the fault of the free market but of your fellow citizens—and perhaps of your own failure to convince them to alter their behavior!

Road Maps, Street Signs, and Market Prices

The free market is based on private property. What is traded during a sale is one piece of private property, usually a product, for another piece of private property, namely, money. When people trade money for goods (or services), they establish free-market prices for them. Free-market prices reflect the size and intensity of "demand" by consumers for the goods and services as well as the amount of "supply." One does not have to even take an economics course to understand that when a product is popular and people are lining up to buy it, the price is likely to go up, and vice versa—when fewer and fewer people want it, the product becomes cheaper as a result.

In such a scenario the higher price serves as a signal to existing and potential competitors in the business that there is money to be made. The businesses respond to that signal as profit-seeking businesses always do, by producing and offering for sale even more of the popular product. The key here is that the businesses don't necessarily need to know why the product is popular, only that consumers want it and that that desire has driven up the price. They may make a good profit temporarily, but all the competition and increased supply will eventually cause the price (and profit levels) to drop, maybe even below where it started. In the end, the wishes of consumers are satisfied by all the profit-hungry businesses as though they were led by an invisible hand.

Speaking of hands, on the other hand everyone knows that when any valued resource becomes scarce it is a good idea to conserve it and use less of it to prevent it from running out altogether. Fortunately, we do not need an energy czar to tell us when to reduce our energy consumption—or a car czar, a water czar, a lumber czar, a grocery czar, or any other kind of czar or economic dictator. Whenever any resource—natural or man-made—becomes more scarce, that scarcity will be reflected in a higher price for that resource. It is the higher price that informs us that we should cut back and not use as much of it, or seek out substitutes. When the gasoline price increases by, say, a dollar a gallon, millions of people will respond by carpooling to work and school, taking a bus, doing less leisure driving, or, if given enough time, even moving closer to work and eliminating their commute altogether. Again, we as consumers do not necessarily need to know why gasoline is more expensive, only that it is: the higher price is a signal that tells us that we should reduce our consumption of it and conserve that resource.

But wait! There's also a third hand (kind of creepy, I know). Another essential function of prices in a free market is that they instruct manufacturers of products and providers of services about what materials to use to produce the product or service in the most efficient (and profitable) manner. Every production process can involve many different types of "inputs" in producing the final "output," which is a clunky economics term for products and services that we spend our money on. How do businesspeople decide how to organize production? Well, by 1) finding "inputs" of comparable quality, and 2) choosing to use the cheapest one. Only free-market prices can tell them which input to choose.

In a nutshell, free-market prices are like street signs that guide us in our economic decision-making, whether we are acting as consumers or product or service providers. Living in an economy without private property and free-market prices would be like trying to find your way around a strange city with no street signs and no map to tell you where anything is. It would be sheer chaos, which of course is what happened in socialist countries that abolished private property and free-market prices in the twentieth century.

Free-market prices based on private property and private enterprise are essential and indeed imperative if a society values economic freedom in particular and human freedom in general, and seeks to provide opportunities for prosperity to all who wish to pursue them. That is exactly the reason why the first of the ten "planks" in *The Communist Manifesto* by Karl Marx and Friedrich Engels, which laid out a strategy for *destroying* economic freedom (a.k.a. "capitalism"), was, in all capital letters: "ABOLITION OF PRIVATE PROPERTY."

CHAPTER 2

The Worst Economic Idea in the World

The worst economic idea in the world is for politicians rather than buyers and sellers to set prices for goods and services. The politicization of prices is a recipe for the destruction of economic prosperity, which of course is why it was a key component of twentieth-century socialism. Socialism was—and is—always about what economist Ludwig von Mises called "destructionism" first and foremost.[1] The existing economic system of capitalism must first be destroyed, socialists have always preached, before their alleged socialist utopia can be created. The failure to allow the free market to set prices is precisely the reason twentieth-century socialism (and socialism in any century) was such a miserable, life-destroying failure. Without the guidance of free-market prices, the Russian socialists had no idea in the world how to efficiently organize production. Consequently, in more than seventy years they never produced a single consumer product that anyone would say was world-leader—or even mediocre, for that matter.

Your author recalls teaching an MBA class at Loyola University in Baltimore in the early 1990s and asking the class if anyone could think of any such successful product produced by Soviet socialism. A U.S. Army

A Book You're Not Supposed to Read

Ludwig von Mises, *Socialism: An Economic and Sociological Analysis* (Indianapolis: Liberty Classics, 2008).

In this prescient book, originally published in 1922, the year the Soviet Union was founded, Mises explained why socialism could never work as a viable economic system and could only produce poverty and misery. History has proven that he was right and the socialists were wrong.

officer from the Aberdeen Proving Ground offered the example of Soviet AK-47s, while another student said "caviar." Well, the latter is produced by a *fish*—the sturgeon, which almost became extinct from the horrific pollution in the Soviet Union—whereas there is no way of knowing how many resources went into producing the Russian AK-47s—which after all were a military rather than a consumer product in the first instance—since there were no financial statements of costs and profits and losses under socialism. The iconic Soviet rifles had to be priced like similar weapons on the world market, but the Russians likely lost money on every one that was sold, with their

★ ★ ★

Robbery under Law

Washington politicians have even perfected a legal extortion scam (immoral but not illegal, since it benefits the lawmakers themselves) whereby they threaten to impose price ceilings (government-mandated prices lower than the free-market price) in a particular industry, until the threatened industry floods congressional campaign coffers with "donations." After sufficient "donations" are banked, the proposed price ceilings are then forgotten. Legal scholar Fred S. McChesney authored an entire Harvard University Press book about this form of legalized extortion entitled *Money*

for Nothing: Politics, Rent Extraction, and Political Extortion.[2] In it he gives chapter and verse of how this racket is operated, with proposed legislation dubbed "milker bills" by congressional staffers because they are intended to "milk" political "contributions" from the targeted industries. McChesney gives examples of how price controls were threatened by Congress on the cable television and pharmaceutical industries, for example, and then dropped after millions in campaign contributions were pocketed by both major political parties.

costs far exceeding the price that each weapon could fetch.

Not all advocates of allowing prices to be dictated by politicians are socialist ideologues. In fact, most are just your typical, garden-variety politicians who are happy to control prices as a means of dispensing political favors to potential voters to help themselves keep their jobs. A politician can, for example, curry favor with renters and get their votes by promising cheaper rent by means of rent-control laws that keep apartment rental prices below the market. In another instance, he can curry favor with farmers and get kickbacks (known as "campaign contributions") from them by supporting higher food prices via "price support" laws, which are always especially harmful to the poor who, like everyone else, must pay more for food but, unlike everyone else, really can't afford it.

A Book You're Not Supposed to Read

Fred McChesney, *Money for Nothing: Politics, Rent Extraction, and Political Extortion* (Cambridge: Harvard University Press, 1997).

How politicians operate a legalized extortion racket by threatening price controls unless sufficient "campaign contributions" are forthcoming.

Concocting Economic Chaos

For as long as there have been politicians, they have banked on the economic ignorance of the general public by promising something for nothing. Price ceilings—government-mandated prices set below free-market prices—are just one of myriad tricks that politicians have up their sleeves in this regard.

Everyone wants cheaper stuff, but when governments mandate lower prices it creates economic chaos that can sometimes literally become deadly and life-threatening. Free-market competition, entrepreneurship, and business expansion and creation—not the machinations of vote-seeking politicians—is how the products and services that we all make use of and enjoy become cheaper and cheaper (and of better quality) over time. Government-mandated lower prices affect both sides of any market: the lower price increases the amount that people want to buy while at the same time the amount supplied to the market declines, as the price is pushed below the cost to some businesses of supplying the product to the market. When more people want something that is in lower and lower supply, the result is *shortages*. What good is it that a bottle of water, for example, is cheaper if there is no bottled water left at the grocery store?! That is exactly what happens over and over again after hurricanes or other natural disasters disrupt cities and towns in their wake. (There is nothing natural about the disaster when it is created by government price controls.)

When the power goes out after a hurricane—and sometimes stays out for days or even weeks—people tend to go out and try to stockpile bottled water and other necessities. The explosion of demand increases the price of these items, which in turn incentivizes others to make money by supplying more of the higher-priced water and other items. This assures that the price will eventually go down, and the shortages will be resolved—eventually everyone can get all the water he needs, even if at a temporarily higher price.

However, politicians routinely stick their noses into this process by imposing "anti–price gouging" laws and regulations—a euphemism for "price ceilings." Such laws and regulations usually stipulate that the price for water, for example, must be no higher than it was before the hurricane. The result is quintessentially predictable because it is the same result that has occurred hundreds of times: when governments force down prices when demand for a product is skyrocketing, they destroy the incentive for greater supply to appear quickly on the market, while stimulating consumer demand even further, generating shortages with increased demand and decreased supplies. The water may—and often does—completely run out during the crisis. Thanks a lot, Mr. and Mrs. virtue-signaling politician.

Sometimes politicians add fuel to the economic fires they create by responding to the failures of their own price-control policies by doubling down with even more price controls. For example, after price ceilings in an industry (predictably) cause shortages of the product, politicians often refuse to take responsibility for the problems that *they* created and instead impose additional price ceilings on "inputs"—the materials, labor, and so forth that are used to produce the price-controlled product. They mistakenly believe that that will return the product's manufacturer to profitability, but all they do is create more shortages, this time in the input markets! The producers will find that they literally cannot physically produce adequate quantities of the product to meet the consumer demand because of the government-created shortages of inputs! If the politicians go far enough and impose price ceilings on *all* inputs, they will have completely created an island of socialism (under the classic definition of government control over the means of production).[3]

Government-imposed price ceilings can also lead to bribery and corruption. Since they create shortages, some means other than ability to pay must be used to determine who gets the limited supply of the product or service. A classic example would be the effects of price ceilings in the form of rent-control laws implemented in parts of New York City after World War II. Rent-control laws always create housing shortages by stimulating demand while making it less profitable to be in the rental apartment business. What happened in New York City is that something called "key money" arose. Landlords would say to prospective renters: The government prohibits me from charging more than $200 a month for this beautiful apartment overlooking Central Park, so that will be the monthly rent. Just give me $15,000 for the key, and the apartment is yours.

Needless to say, only the more affluent could afford the "key money," so it was the rich who benefited from rent control in New York, even though the rent control was—as always—sold by the politicians as a means of helping the poor. Among well-known people who have benefited from rent control are millionaire actress Mia Farrow, who had a rent-controlled apartment in New York City for years. She paid approximately $2,500 per month in an area where rents were typically three to four times that amount (the apartment was featured in the Woody Allen movie *Manhattan*); former California governor Jerry Brown, who lived in a rent-controlled apartment in Sacramento, California; and singer Cyndi Lauper, among others. "Celebrities Love New York Rent Control," as the Frontier Centre for Public Policy explained.[4]

Sometimes key money is not enough to make the rental apartment business profitable, so landlords cut back in the one area where they still have some latitude to increase their profits: building maintenance. Owning rental properties involves maintenance expenses of all kinds. Rent-control laws give landlords incentives to cut back or eliminate maintenance altogether to eke out a profit. The losers are the tenants who must live in increasingly dilapidated apartments. Sometimes landlords just throw in the towel and abandon the properties altogether, turning them into squalid squatter hovels. On top of that, rent control is also a signal to real estate developers not to even think about investing in rental housing—causing even greater housing shortages, especially if there is an expanding population of renters. Or rental housing will be converted into non-price-controlled condominiums and sold to more affluent residents, causing an ever-bigger shortage in rental housing. Price controls always and everywhere cause economic chaos and misery.

When politicians are not buying votes and soliciting campaign donations by mandating lower prices, they are buying votes and soliciting campaign donations by mandating *higher* prices in the form of price floors—government-mandated prices above the normal free-market price. Such policies have been prevalent in agricultural markets since at least the 1920s, when they were first championed by President Herbert Hoover and then expanded upon by his successor, FDR. Like price ceilings, price floors are a political gimmick designed to gain votes and campaign donations from a special-interest group at the expense of everyone else.

In the case of agricultural price floors, the special-interest group that benefits is farmers, who want to sell their crops at a higher price. The losers are all the rest of us, who have to pay higher prices for food. It works as a political trick because the farmers shower politicians with campaign donations and votes, whereas the average consumer is clueless as to why bread, milk, and steak are a little more expensive than last year. If anything, they will blame "greedy corporations." But corporations are always greedy. It is silly to believe that there are sudden bursts of greed where there were none before, or that greed is, say, 50 percent higher this year than it was last year—before the price floors were implemented—and that it is the increased greed that explains the higher prices.

Farmers and food distributors can charge higher prices thanks to price floors, but they can't force us to buy their products. As long as not all food items are affected by price floors, we consumers can just buy less of the higher-priced regulated food items and more of other foods. While the effect of price floors is to induce farmers to produce more crops—they will plant more acres of soybeans, for example, if government imposes a 50 percent mandated price increase for soybeans—the "law of demand" tells us that at the higher price, consumers will purchase fewer soybeans and soybean products. The combination of increased supply and fewer soybean purchases will therefore cause surpluses. These are the quantities of farm goods to which people have said, "No thanks, not at that price." Thus, as a result of price floors, millions of tons of food rot away in silos, or—to add insult to injury to the taxpayers and consumers—the government uses tax dollars to buy up the surpluses and gives them away as "foreign aid" to developing countries, playing the role of international Santa Claus. Government is effectively saying to consumers: "You refuse to buy the surplus soybeans, wheat, corn, or whatever that we have created with our price floors but we, being the government, will *force* you to pay for it anyway and give it away as foreign aid."

Then what often happens is that the dumping of millions of tons of grain in a poor country through "foreign aid" causes the price of grain there to approach zero, driving the country's farmers out of business and forcing them to move to the cities, where there is often already high unemployment, in order to find work. Price controls always and everywhere cause economic chaos and misery.

FDR's Boneheaded Scheme to Make Everything More Expensive during the Great Depression

President Franklin D. Roosevelt's so-called "brain trust" of Ivy League professors convinced him of the rather brainless idea that the Great Depression was caused by low prices; therefore, it could be ended by government-mandated *high* prices. Consequently, in 1933 and 1934 what historians call the "first New Deal" involved dozens of new laws designed to increase the price of almost everything—manufactured goods as well as farm crops and livestock. Corporations were on board, of course, since they knew that trying to raise prices by forming price-fixing cartels rarely worked and in any case was illegal under the antitrust laws anyway. Roosevelt's National Industrial Recovery Administration (NIRA) did the cartel price-fixing for them!

The National Industrial Recovery Act of 1933 (NIRA) was an economic monstrosity, employing thousands of "code enforcement" police who roamed the country threatening fines (or worse) to businesses committing the "crime" of cutting prices to try to stimulate a little business. More than seven hundred categories of industries and businesses were prohibited from charging prices below the "cost of production." However, there was a lot of lying about what true costs of production were, allowing many businesses to charge sky-high prices, just as Roosevelt wanted. Journalist John T. Flynn wrote at the time about how FDR's code police in New York City "roamed through the garment district like storm troopers. They could enter a man's factory, send him out, line up his employees, subject them to minute interrogation, take over his books.... Night work was forbidden. Flying squadrons of these private coat-and-suit police went through the district at night, battering down doors with axes looking for men who were committing the crime of sewing together a pair of pants at night."[5]

A Book You're Not Supposed to Read

John T. Flynn, *The Roosevelt Myth* (New York: Fox and Wilkes, 1998).

The truth about how the "New Deal" was little different from German and Italian economic fascism.

In essence, FDR's price floors created dozens or hundreds of monopolies in the middle of the Great Depression. And as any economics student should know, monopolies tend to restrict production and charge higher prices. Higher prices may be good *for the monopoly*—at least for a while—but it is bad for consumers. The NIRA was a gigantic rob-Peter-to-pay-Paul scheme— in other words, a scheme that impoverished the average working-class American even further. And the restricted production reduced employment, causing the unemployment rate to be even *higher* than it otherwise would have been. Thankfully, the U.S. Supreme Court ruled in 1935 that the National Industrial Recovery Act was unconstitutional.[6]

Price Controls = Legalized Theft

That price controls are a bald-faced act of legalized theft, or "legal plunder" as the French economic journalist Frederic Bastiat called them,[7] is demonstrated by one of the very first U.S. Supreme Court cases dealing

A Book You're Not Supposed to Read

Frederic Bastiat, *The Law* (Auburn, Alabama: Mises Institute, 2008).

The greatest economic journalist of the nineteenth century explains the importance of limited constitutional government in limiting "legal plunder" and its destructive effects on prosperity and civil government.

with price controls. The 1876 case *Munn v. Illinois* involved a grain storage business owned by the two Munn brothers, who were victims of political predation by the powerful Midwest farm lobby known at the time as "the Granger movement."[8] The Grangers had managed to get the Illinois legislature to pass a law imposing price ceilings on grain storage and transportation. There was no rationale for such a law—other than the fact that the Grangers had enough political power to enable them to plunder fellow citizens such as the Munns. And so they did, forcing the brothers to accept less than what farmers were voluntarily willing to pay them on the free market to store the grain. The only difference between that law and armed robbery of the Munn brothers is that in the latter case a firearm would have been involved. Either way, the Munns were *forced* to hand over money to strangers for nothing in return. It was an attack on the very principle of private property of the kind the founding fathers, especially James Madison, the "father of the Constitution," feared. The whole purpose of the Constitution, Madison wrote in the famous *Federalist* no. 10, was to limit or eliminate such majority-rule tyranny, which he called "the violence of faction."[9]

Munn v. Illinois is considered to be a watershed Supreme Court case because it began the process of the complete repudiation of Madison and the other founders' constitutional protections of private property. It was "justified" by the most circular reasoning ever mumbled by a Supreme Court justice: Chief Justice Morrison Waite claimed that any private property that is "subject to public use" can and should be regulated by the state "in the public interest." That, of course, would include all private property of any kind imaginable, opening the door to the legalization of what is essentially socialism, or the total government control of the means of production through regulation. It is important to note that in this specific case there was no regulation "in the public interest." The grain storage price ceiling law was strictly a piece of special-interest legislation that effectively plundered and stole from the Munn brothers for no other reason than to enrich a more politically powerful group in Illinois. It was exactly the kind of rotten, corrupt "violence of faction" that James Madison warned could eventually cause the death of democracy itself, if taken too far. As Madison wrote, governments that failed to control "the violence of faction" have "everywhere been destroyed."[10]

Four Thousand Years of Price-Control Chaos

Governments have been creating economic chaos with price controls for four thousand years! In *Forty Centuries of Wage and Price Controls*, authors Robert Schuettinger and Eamonn Butler surveyed the imposition of price controls beginning with ancient Egypt and found that the results have always been the same: economic chaos, shortages, and even revolutions.[11] They note that in ancient Egypt state intervention in economic affairs, including the governmental dictation of all prices, was omnipresent. As is always the case with price controls, this required "an army of inspectors."[12] Imposing price ceilings on food to gain favor with the populace, the Egyptian government caused many farmers simply to leave their farms. By the end of the third century BC the entire

A Book You're Not Supposed to Read

Robert Schuettinger and Eamonn Butler, *Forty Centuries of Wage and Price Controls* (Auburn, Alabama: Mises Institute, 2014).

A history of how politicians have been creating poverty, misery, and economic chaos with price controls for more than four thousand years. Will the public *ever* catch on?

Egyptian economy collapsed as a result, as did the nation's political stability.

More than four thousand years ago in Babylon, the famous Code of Hammurabi was "in reality a maze of price control regulations." "If a man hire a field-labourer, he shall give him eight gur of corn per annum," dictated the code. "If a man hire a herdsman, he shall give him six gur of corn per annum."[13] Such laws "smothered economic progress for centuries," write Schuettinger and Butler, but there was remarkable growth once the code was abandoned.[14]

Ancient Athens also imposed price-control laws, with the death penalty attached for violators—something that Adolf Hitler would adopt centuries later in Nazi Germany. Greece's saving grace was that not enough government enforcers were employed, which allowed for flourishing black markets to get around the shortages of just about everything caused by the price controls.[15]

George Washington's army nearly starved to death in the field because of price controls on food imposed by Pennsylvania and other colonial governments. Just about everything needed for the army in the field disappeared as a result of shortages created by the price ceilings. The Continental Congress wisely adopted an anti–price control resolution on June 4, 1778, calling on all the several states to "suspend all laws limiting, regulating or restraining the price of any article."[16] Within a few months, as it became profitable once again for local merchants to produce and deliver food, clothing, and everything else the army needed, George Washington's army was "well provided for."[17]

The hated Law of the Maximum in the French Revolution was another version of a price-ceiling law. Imposed on grain and myriad other foods, it caused a starvation crisis, with people literally collapsing in the streets from hunger. Thousands died from this particular government decree. When Robespierre was being dragged through the streets on way to his execution, the crowds were shouting, "There goes the dirty Maximum!"[18]

Price Controls Always Cause *Higher* Prices in the End

Price floors like the ones imposed on certain agricultural products are intended to make food more expensive (and line the pockets of politically connected farm corporations). Price ceilings, on the other hand, are sold to the public with the promise of holding prices down. Exactly the opposite is the truth—in the long run. By making markets less profitable, price ceilings deter incentives to produce and sell. Consequently, when the price ceilings are lifted, as they almost always are eventually, prices typically fall, contrary to all the politicians' promises, and the shortages and other forms of economic chaos caused by the price ceilings disappear.

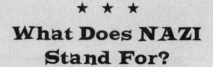

★ ★ ★
What Does NAZI Stand For?

After all, it was the German National *Socialist* Workers' Party. The Nazis were "national socialists," as opposed to the Russian *international* socialists. They had officially nationalized about half of all German industry, with the other half de facto nationalized through pervasive command-and-control regulation of all aspects of the German economy.

One famous example of this phenomenon is how economist Ludwig Erhard, the German minister of economic affairs after World War II, ended all of the Nazi price controls in 1948, initiating the "German economic miracle." Erhard was a World War I veteran who had lived through the German hyperinflation of the 1920s and earned a Ph.D. in economics. He was a critic of the Nazi regime from the very beginning, as much as criticism was permitted. In 1942 he composed an essay advocating a free society and a free market in Germany after the war, for which the Nazis kicked him out of his job.[19]

After the war, the American and British occupation authorities appointed Erhard as the head of something called the Bizonal Economic Council, and later minister of economic affairs. Hitler had imposed pervasive price controls on just about everything in 1936, with price ceilings to (supposedly) hold down the cost of everything needed for his military. The Roosevelt administration had implemented similar economic policies.

Since the Nazi economic regulations were essentially the same as FDR's New Deal policies and the British Labour Party's Fabian socialist policies, the occupation authorities kept them in place after the war. By 1948 there was still no economic recovery to speak of in Germany, primarily because the Nazi price controls, extremely high income taxes, high import tariffs, and other regulations were still stifling economic freedom as much as they had under the Hitler regime.

On June 19, 1948, Erhard went on the radio and announced an end to all price controls in Germany, replaced the occupation authorities' rationing coupons (similar to ones used in the United States under FDR's price-control regime), and cut income taxes and tariff rates. General Lucius Clay, in charge of the occupation authorities, is said to have stormed into Erhard's office and accused him of changing the price controls without proper permission. Erhard responded to the general that he had not *changed* the price controls but *abolished* them!

FDR had died, and the New Dealers, who had approved of all the Nazi economic regulations, were no longer in charge. The U.S. and British governments apparently just threw up their hands and allowed Erhard to create a free market in Germany. Economic activity immediately picked up as the famous German work ethic kicked in and quickly created prosperity that was dubbed the "German economic miracle."

But it was *not* a miracle, just economic common sense that anyone who, like Erhard, had studied economics even for a short while (unlike the economically ignorant Nazi socialists) would know about. By the early 1960s German economic growth was not far behind that of the United States, and the rest is history.

A similar but nearly as dramatic instance of prosperity-boosting deregulation happened in the United States when Presidents Carter and Reagan deregulated the oil and gas and airline industries in the late 1970s and early 1980s. President Carter started the deregulation of these industries near the end of his term in office, and President Reagan followed through with it on a much quicker timetable. One of the very first things Reagan did after taking the oath of office was sign an executive order for the immediate deregulation of oil and gas prices. The effect was exactly what any college freshman introductory economics student (but not the *New York Times* or *Washington Post* editorial writers) would expect: prices went up for a very short time, followed by an explosion of supply and fierce competition in the newly freed markets, causing a vast expansion of production and *declining* prices. The price of a barrel of crude oil was $130.39 in 1979, for instance, but it plunged to $26.14 by 1986 and to $20.08 by 1998.[21] This radical price drop was reflected in less expensive gasoline, natural gas, and heating oil prices.

Since the New Deal of the 1930s, the commercial airline industry had operated as a government-managed monopoly or cartel, with the federal government's Civil Aeronautics Board (CAB) setting all prices and routes, among other things. The CAB was a classic example of "regulatory capture"—the phenomenon in which a regulatory agency is "captured" by the industry it is supposed to be regulating in the public interest. Instead, it regulated the airline industry for the benefit of the airline industry and against the consumers' interests. Price competition was literally banned. The airlines responded with competition on quality, such as offering "free" alcohol and food. The government regulators then even regulated the size of sandwiches that could be offered on flights—too much competition!

That all ended thanks to Presidents Carter and Reagan, and the result was once again predictable to any eighteen-year-old first-year economics student: the creation of a competitive free market and the death of the old New Deal airline industry monopoly scheme reduced air fares dramatically. All of a sudden there were such things as "super saver fares" and even the creation of new, discount airlines like what today is Southwest Airlines. Such competition had been banned by the CAB, under whose regulation there were fewer commercial airline companies competing in 1975 than there had been in 1935.[22]

Like Ludwig Erhard, Presidents Carter and Reagan ignored the pleadings and predictions of the economically ignorant and the politically conniving politicians who were promising the public something for nothing in the form of price controls. They relied instead on economic common sense, as politically incorrect as it may have been at the time, to the great benefit of their fellow citizens.

CHAPTER 3

The Nirvana Fallacy in Economics
(Or, How to Attack a Straw-Man Argument)

Until the time of the New Deal of the 1930s, economists thought about the concept of competition pretty much like the average citizen did: businesses compete for customer loyalty by constantly striving to keep costs and prices as low as possible, innovating to provide a better product or service than their competitors, holding sales or offering rebates, creating new products and services in hopes that they will catch on, providing good customer service, and even merging with other businesses to produce at a larger level of volume and achieve "economies of scale" (low costs per unit from, for example, mass production on Henry Ford's famous assembly line).[1]

To the older generations of economists from Adam Smith on, competition was a dynamic, ongoing process of entrepreneurship whereby businesses were forced to innovate, cut prices, create new products, cut costs, advertise, and more—or else. Failure to do these things leads to losses or bankruptcy in a competitive marketplace. Success at doing these things is the key to creating prosperity for business owners and their families, their employees, investors, and communities.

But starting roughly in the 1930s, the leading lights of the economics profession adopted a new theory of competition. Actual, real-world competition had not changed significantly, but the *theory* of competition taught by the economics profession did. Anyone anywhere in the world who took an introductory university course in economics from the 1940s and throughout the next forty years was likely to have been taught from a textbook entitled *Economics* by MIT professor Paul Samuelson, or one of its several clones.

Paul Samuelson's book and several close imitators dominated economic education for decades. It is said to have sold over four million copies from its first edition in 1948 to the late 1980s, when more free market–oriented textbooks finally appeared.

As an indication of Samuelson's liberal or even socialist bias, in the 1988 edition of his famous textbook he stated that it had been proven that a socialist economy like the Soviet Union's "can thrive" and predicted that the Soviet economy would become larger than the U.S. economy in terms of GDP by the year 2000. The next year the Berlin Wall fell, and two years later the Soviet Union collapsed altogether—with an economy that was probably no more than 5 percent the size of the U.S. economy. In fact, Samuelson had habitually overestimated the size of the Soviet economy in his textbook for the previous twenty-seven years.[2]

On the subject of competition, Samuelson and all the other like-minded textbook authors taught the new theory of "perfect competition." Students were disabused of the commonsense understanding of competition—it was not simply the never-ending efforts to cater to the consuming public's ever-changing whims and fancies. Instead, they were fed a series of assumptions about what a *perfectly* competitive world—an economic utopia or nirvana—would look like.

That never-to-be-realized-anywhere-on-earth state of perfect competition is one where all products in every industry are identical; they are produced by "many" business firms; everyone charges the same price; everyone has perfect information—consumers are assumed to be essentially omniscient about all the possible opportunities before them, and businesses are equally omniscient about how to produce products and services at the lowest possible costs; and there is free or costless entry into every industry and exit out of it. Several other equally unrealistic assumptions were added over the years, but these were always the main ones. This pipe dream became the new understanding of what constituted "competition," at least among academic economists. Samuelson taught that the only really competitive industries in America were in such things as cotton and natural gas, which are of course very homogeneous products! Every other industry, he taught several generations of college students, suffered from some degree of monopoly and was therefore in need of government regulation.

The older generations of economic scholars, equipped with a very different understanding of competition, were generally supportive of economic freedom, free markets, and laissez-faire. So much so that when the U.S. Congress passed its first antitrust or anti-monopoly law, the 1890 Sherman Antitrust Act, nearly everyone who was employed as an economist opposed the law as a matter of principle because they understood that the law inherently conflicted with the ongoing process of competition and entrepreneurship.[3] At the time mergers, for example, were viewed as basically good for society because they almost universally led to *lower* prices for consumers. An "antitrust" law that blocked mergers was therefore understood to be likely to cause *higher* prices and was anti-competitive.

That all changed radically with the new theory of "perfect" competition. All of a sudden, economists began declaring that markets were "failing"

A Book You're Not Supposed to Read

Dominick Armentano, *Antitrust and Monopoly: Anatomy of a Policy Failure* (New York: Wiley, 1983).

For over a century, guided by a wrong-headed theory of competition, government protected competitors from competition instead of protecting consumers from monopoly. It prosecuted businesses for cutting costs and prices, creating new and successful products, expanding production, and increasing employment while doing so.

everywhere, and those supposed failures required government intervention (always assumed to be perfectly effective, of course, led by wise and nearly omniscient "public servants" and their academic economic advisors). What a coincidence that this new theory of competition was perfectly in sync with the Roosevelt administration's main ideological and political theme—that the Great Depression had been caused by a breakdown of competitive capitalism, which needed to be saved from itself by hyper-interventionist government.

All these supposed "market failures" were simply examples of real-world markets not matching up with assumptions of the perfect competition model. Businesses did not in fact produce products and services that were identical to those of their competitors. Product innovation resulted in very heterogenous product lines. Businesses did not all charge the exact same prices—they tried to compete with volume discounts and periodic sales, and sometimes charged higher prices in response to surges in consumer demand, usually fueled by the popularity of a product or service. Mergers often did result in fewer businesses competing in a single industry.

The "perfect information" assumption led to theories about how advertising was unnecessary. If consumers are assumed to know everything, why would there be a need for advertising?! Advertisements were assumed to serve no other function than to increase the costs of doing business, causing prices to rise and creating "barriers to entry" to potential new competitors who might not be able to afford expensive advertising campaigns. Or advertising was subtle brainwashing that convinced people to spend their money on things they didn't really want. That money, economists such as Harvard's John Kenneth Galbraith said, would be better used if it was taxed and spent by government instead. Galbraith essentially spent his entire half-century career at Harvard making this argument in book after book.[4]

For decades, the "many firms" assumption was used to justify government prohibitions of corporate mergers—since two firms merging into one does in fact cause one less business firm to exist. Antitrust (that is, anti-monopoly) policy thus became a numbers game, in which hugely expensive government lawsuits filed by the Federal Trade Commission, the Antitrust Division of the U.S. Department of Justice, and state attorneys general were ongoing for decades.

The "free entry" assumption of the perfect competition model led to myriad theories about "barriers to entry" into industry because, after all, nothing is free in the real world, including the cost of entering any industry—from renting a kiosk at the local mall to constructing a new automobile factory. This, too, was used as a rationale for government intervention to block mergers, to regulate or prohibit some forms of advertising, and to interfere with many other ordinary business practices under the theory that because they were not costless, they were creating some kind of monopolistic barrier to entry into the industry.

At around the same time that the perfect competition model became accepted dogma in the interventionist mainstream of the economics profession, a new theory of "monopolistic competition" was invented by British economist Joan Robinson and American economist Edward Chamberlin.[5] The two main books authored by these two government intervention–minded economists were very similar. They both conceded that yes, most manufacturing industries of their day *were* comprised of "many" business firms in competition with one another, in keeping with the "many firms" assumption of the perfect competition theory. However, they often employed a strategy of "product differentiation" or, worse yet, advertised to create a *perception* that their product was different from all others, even if it was

A Book You're Not Supposed to Read

Yale Brozen, *Concentration, Mergers, and Public Policy* (New York: MacMillan, 1982).

The University of Chicago economist surveys the voluminous Chicago School literature proving that mergers tend to decrease costs and prices to consumers, while blocking them does the opposite.

not physically very different. If a tire manufacturer produced slightly thicker and longer-lasting tires, for example, then while the company might have a hundred competitors in the tire business, it still had "monopoly power" as the only seller of a unique product. If tires are defined as precisely as possible, then the tire industry can be viewed as being plagued with "monopoly" everywhere, despite the outward appearance of "many" competitors! This too novel theory was used to advocate for yet more antitrust regulation of business. The level of regulation eventually got so out of control that during the Carter administration in the late 1970s the Democrat-controlled Congress threatened to defund the Federal Trade Commission because its regulations were severely stifling and handicapping American industry, causing even higher unemployment in the midst of an already-severe recession.

Enough with the Nirvana Fallacy Already!

Three decades or so of "market failure" theorizing were based on comparing the assumptions of "perfect competition" theory with the actual real world and discovering: Aha! The industrial world is not as perfect as our theory says it should be! It is not like heaven on earth! It therefore fails and needs to be improved upon or saved—by the always-perfect government bureaucracy!

In 1969 UCLA economics professor Harold Demsetz addressed this obviously biased straw-man-argument approach to the study of markets in a peer-reviewed academic journal article in which he coined the phrase "the Nirvana Fallacy": comparing the real word to an impossible-to-ever-attain nirvana or utopia, and then condemning the real world as "failed" or "imperfect."[6] Everything in the real world is imperfect, of course, so this method of analysis was (and is) indeed fraudulent and dishonest. The entire mainstream of the economics profession had been dishonestly spinning straw-man arguments for decades to justify massive government regulation and control of industry.

Only the Austrian School economists, led by Ludwig von Mises, F. A. Hayek, Henry Hazlitt, and Murray N. Rothbard, never accepted this unrealistic and frankly shady method of analysis. They continued to analyze and study competition understood as a dynamic, rivalrous process of entrepreneurship and not as a set of arbitrary and unrealistic assumptions.

Thankfully, a large portion of the academic economics profession eventually came to its senses regarding the topic of product differentiation and decided that government-enforced "homogenous products" are not such a good idea after all. The absurdity of a federal antitrust lawsuit against General Mills, General Foods, Quaker Oats, and Kellogg's in 1972 was a likely catalyst for introducing a dose of sanity.[8] In what is known as "the Cereals Case," the Federal Trade Commission (FTC) accused these four companies of operating a "shared monopoly" in dry cereal because the four of them together had a 90 percent share of the total market for dry cereal. It was a crime, the FTC alleged, that these four companies had introduced more than just plain cornflakes in their product lines, and lo and behold, their customers liked the new cereals and ate them up—literally. The enormous popularity of their newer brands of ready-to-eat breakfast foods was awarded with that 90 percent market share. The four cereal companies were essentially being punished for pleasing their

★ ★ ★

Competition Is Anti-Competitive

Nobel laureate F. A. Hayek summarized the Austrian School critique of "market failure" based on the perfect competition theory with a single sentence in an essay entitled "The Meaning of Competition": "In perfect competition there is no competition," Hayek wrote.[7] He pointed out that all of the ordinary components of ordinary business competition such as price cutting, advertising, and product differentiation are *assumed away* by the perfect competition theory. In fact, in a jumble of Orwellian nonsense, these competitive business practices are branded as monopolistic and *anti*-competitive by the theory—the exact opposite of reality!

customers better than most of their competitors, of which there were many. After a decade of very expensive litigation, the FTC dropped the case. Despite a 90 percent market share among four competitors, none of them was shown to have charged monopolistic prices because, after all, if they did, consumers could easily switch to bacon and eggs, bagels, muffins, pancakes, and a myriad of other alternative breakfast foods.

The Austrian School economists always understood that the main purpose of product differentiation was to create a better fit between what consumers want and what exists for sale in the marketplace.[9] The surest way to make money, after all, is to give the customers what they want. The mindset of *give me what I want, and I will give you what you want* is the best recipe for business success. The proliferation of products is in actuality a sign of competitiveness, just the opposite of what was taught for decades by prestigious economists at Cambridge (such as Joan Robinson) and Harvard (Edward Chamberlin).

The 1998 annual report of the Federal Reserve Bank of Dallas was titled "The Right Stuff: America's Move to Mass Customization." "Mass customization" is the integration of mass production with computer technology in a way that has made it profitable for businesses to create a proliferation of product and service offerings for ever-fickle consumers.[10] Previously, during the "machine age," the way to make big money was to produce standardized products in large volume to take advantage of economies of scale. "Niche markets" were rare. The report was a final-nail-in-the-coffin kind of study for the once-dominant condemnation of product differentiation. The report made the point that it was a *good* thing for competition that there were 1,212 vehicle styles in 1998 compared to 654 styles 25 years earlier; that there were 192 SUV styles compared to 18; almost 5 million websites; 15 TV screen sizes compared to 5; 340 breakfast cereals compared to 160; 285 types of running shoe compared to just 5; 31 brands of bicycles compared to 8; and so on. Since customer preferences are so widely differentiated, industries that produce many differentiated products to match those customer preferences are acting in an efficient and competitive manner, not a monopolistic one.

Should Lower Prices Be Outlawed?

The "homogenous prices" assumption of perfect competition theory gave life to an old superstition that goes by the rubric of "predatory pricing." Folklore, which probably began with the late nineteenth-century "muckraking" journalists, has it that the wealthy industrialists of the day, such as John D. Rockefeller, accumulated at least some of their great wealth through "predatory pricing." According to this notion a big business that is said to have a "war chest" of profits will cut its price below its own average cost of producing its product, intentionally losing money on every sale. This is said to have caused smaller competitors with higher costs to go out of business. It might take many years, but the predator is assumed to eventually drive everyone else out of the market, at which point he will charge sky-high monopolistic prices indefinitely. Rockefeller's Standard Oil Company was said to have cut its prices on refined kerosene and other petroleum products relentlessly for nearly fifty years and become an oil industry "monopolist." (When the U.S. government's antitrust regulators forced Standard Oil to break up into several pieces in 1911, it still had more than three hundred competitors, however).[11]

Economist John McGee explained the irrationality of the theory of "predatory pricing" in a famous (among economists who study such things) case study of the Standard Oil of New Jersey antitrust case published in the prestigious *Journal of Law and Economics* by the University of Chicago. McGee argued that it would have been extremely foolish for John D. Rockefeller—or anyone, for that matter—to have attempted to profit through "predatory pricing." And whatever else may have been said about Rockefeller, he was no fool when it came to making money.

First of all, according to the theory, the "predator" is assumed to be the largest business in the industry and will therefore incur the largest losses of anyone if it is losing money on each and every sale. Second, there is great uncertainty about how long the "price war" will last. One would think that the prospects of an indefinite price war that causes losses year after year would give any business owner pause.

Then there is nothing stopping the "prey" from temporarily shutting down and going on vacation, letting the foolish predator lose all of *his* money by charging prices that cannot cover his costs. And even if the "prey" were bankrupted, there would be nothing stopping other investors from purchasing the prey's assets and reintroducing competition once the predator is charging monopolistic prices. Predatory pricing would then become a strategy of all cost and no benefit. Some strategy!

Another problem with the theory of predatory pricing is that it just assumes that a "war chest" of monopoly profits already exists, *before* a monopoly is created by predatory pricing. It is simply illogical. Any business would have to consider the "opportunity costs" of such a strategy, namely, the other ways of making money that could have been pursued had all those millions not been purposely squandered in a Quixotic crusade to drive every last competitor from the market with years and years of predatory pricing. Would that really be the most profitable avenue? Not likely.[12]

Rockefeller himself was never found guilty of predatory pricing, despite all the folklore about it. In fact, to this day there is no record of any business achieving a monopoly through predatory pricing! There have nevertheless been hundreds, maybe thousands of antitrust lawsuits based on this theory, most of them private lawsuits with one company suing a competitor for lowering its prices. Think about that: in the name of protecting the consumer, antitrust regulation allows businesses to sue to "protect" customers from their competitors' lower prices. Predatory pricing lawsuits are just another protectionist scam designed to thwart competition, not protect it.

At the international level, "dumping" is the word the U.S. government uses for alleged predatory pricing by foreign businesses. A business from overseas that is accused of dumping faces tariffs of up to 100 percent on its products for the "crime" of offering Americans good-quality products at prices that are lower than what is offered anywhere else. Any judge or government bureaucrat who claims that the cheaper prices are part of a predatory-pricing strategy must be claiming mind-reading powers with the ability to know the intentions of the foreign businesses in order to discern that their strategy is to drive every American business from the market—maybe ten years in the future. The only certain result of dumping regulations is to deprive American consumers of the ability to save a few bucks on cheaper goods while lining the pockets of already wealthy American corporations that are protected from international competition. Anti-dumping policy harms one group of Americans (consumers) to create monopolistic profits for another group of Americans (managers, owners, and employees of corporations that are shielded from international competition).

Henry Ford was another famous American capitalist who became wealthy by cutting his prices year after year, but he was anything but a predator. In 1910 Ford's advisors were telling him to follow Buick and Oldsmobile and raise his prices on his Model T automobile. Ford *dropped* his price by 20 percent instead, to $780, which was actually below his average cost. As George Gilder explained Ford's strategy: "Ford set his price not on the basis of his existing costs or sales but on the basis of the much lower costs [due to economies of scale from larger sales volumes] and much expanded sales that might become possible at the lower price. The effect . . . was a 60 percent surge in sales. . . . In the recession year of 1914, he cut prices twice, and sales surged up while other companies failed. By 1916, he had reduced the price of a Model T to $360 and increased his market share from 10 percent to 40 percent. . . . After cutting prices 30 percent during the 1920 economic crisis, Ford commanded a 60 percent share of the market."[13]

Ford himself explained his (non-predatory) price-cutting strategy: "Our policy is to reduce the price, extend the operations, and improve the article. You will note that the reduction in price comes first. We have never considered any costs as fixed. Therefore we first reduce the price to the point where we believe more sales will result. Then we go ahead and try to make the prices.... The new price forces the costs down.... We make more discoveries concerning manufacturing and selling under this forced method than by any method of leisurely investigation."[14]

This means that there are legitimate reasons for temporarily cutting prices below cost, and there is nothing "predatory" about it. It is merely another way of making money by offering consumers better and better products at lower and lower prices in a competitive marketplace.

How Many Is "Many"?

The "many firms" benchmark in the perfect competition theory of competition led to a fifty-year political witch hunt for "monopolies," defined as there being not enough competitors in a given industry to make the government regulators happy. Their witch-hunting weapon of choice was the "concentration ratio." The four-firm concentration ratio, for example, is the percentage of industry sales by the four largest businesses in an industry, according to sales volume. So a four-firm concentration ratio of, say, 60 percent, means that the four most popular businesses in the industry account for 60 percent of all sales in a particular year. Hundreds of antitrust lawsuits were filed based primarily on these ratios, where "industrial concentration" was assumed to be evidence enough of monopoly to launch a federal (or state) lawsuit.

One problem with such a policy is the obvious one of how to determine *why* those four businesses did better than the rest, even if there were dozens of other competitors. As in the dry cereal industry example discussed above, in many instances the answer to this question is simple and straightforward: those businesses, at least at the moment, produce products and charge prices that consumers like better than most others, period. The mere fact of industrial concentration is not by itself proof of a monopoly; it says nothing about how an industry's sales became so concentrated in a relatively few firms.

Moreover, if one or a few businesses are blessed with superior engineering know-how that results in their ability to achieve lower costs and charge lower prices than everyone else, the fact that higher-priced businesses cannot compete and then go out of business is not at all a problem worthy of a federal lawsuit. Economies of scale are another major reason that some industries are "concentrated" according to the government's own definitions. There can also be synergy between two businesses when they combine, taking advantage for example of the superior manufacturing ability of one and the superior marketing talent of the other, creating a stronger company to face international competition. And there is always international competition, regardless of how "concentrated" any domestic American industry might be.

"Merger waves" have occurred in American history—periods in which there are more mergers than usual for a number of years. When such events occur, politicians and pundits stoke fears of monopoly, but they do so out of ignorance. If two businesses in an industry with, say, fifty competitors merge and achieve lower costs and charge lower prices because of economies of scale and gain market share by doing so, there are bound to be imitators among their remaining competitors. Not all of their competitors will succeed in cutting costs and prices, and there is no guarantee that a merger will have that result for anyone, but the point is that merger waves are part of the never-ending *competitive* struggle, not some kind of conspiracy to monopolize the world.

There are no guarantees in business, and many mergers do not work out as planned. However, the individuals involved in the mergers do have much of their own money—and careers—at stake, unlike government regulators who are empowered to allow or disallow mergers but who have not placed one red cent of their own money on the table. If they disallow a merger that would have saved thousands of jobs by allowing the merged company to compete more successfully in international competition, it's no sweat off their backs. There will be no penalties, no losses, no cancellation of promotions, no firings—only an even bigger budget for their government agency next year, and every year thereafter.

Whenever government steps in to break up such mergers, the result is more often than not *higher prices* to consumers, something that antitrust regulation is supposed to deter, not create. Once again, government regulation of industry is used to *increase* prices, harming the average consumer. Moreover, all too often this result is often not just a matter of government bureaucrats' being misinformed about economics. It is no accident. Corporations routinely lobby the government to launch expensive, years-long lawsuits against their competitors when the competitors are gaining market share by cutting their prices, improving their products, or both.[15] Antitrust regulation has long been used as a political bludgeon to thwart competition.

Economist Dominick Armentano did an extensive study of fifty-five of the most famous federal antitrust cases and concluded that *in every single case* the businesses that were prosecuted by the government were cutting prices, innovating, creating new products, improving the quality of their products or services, or some combination of the above.[16] It's hard to believe that this was all just ninety years of making the same mistake over and over again, and not the real purpose of antitrust regulation—to be used as a weapon *against* competition. As Armentano concluded: "Antitrust policy in America is a misleading myth that has served to draw public attention away from the actual process of monopolization that has been occurring throughout the economy. The general public has been deluded into believing that monopoly is a free-market problem, and that the government, through antitrust enforcement, is on the side of the 'angels.' The facts are exactly the opposite. Antitrust…served as a convenient cover for an insidious process of monopolization in the marketplace."[17]

The exact same thing can be said of the "perfect competition" theory as espoused by the mainstream of the academic economics profession for so long, since it provided the intellectual cover for so much competition-destroying antitrust policy.

CHAPTER 4

Bees, Keys, and Externalities

espite Harold Demsetz's exposure of the nirvana fallacy decades ago, economics textbook writers still play the dark game of condemning real-world markets as "imperfect" in myriad ways and recommending government intervention to fix the problem. College students taking an introductory economics course today are bombarded with theories of "market failure" and "imperfections"—under such labels as "externalities," "collusion," "public goods problems," and "asymmetric information" between buyers and sellers. Capitalism is portrayed as one big bundle of failures and imperfections, whereas government is assumed to be composed of enlightened and selfless public-spirited know-it-alls who can and will perfect the economy around us, creating an economic nirvana.

One big problem for the "market failure" theorists, however, is that their writings are long on theory but very short on reality. They sometimes struggle mightily to find a single real-world example to illustrate their theories, and even then it is often discovered that the real-world example is not exactly real after all. A prime example of this phenomenon is the economic theory of "externalities," first associated with early twentieth-century British economist Arthur C. Pigou. In his book *Wealth and Welfare*

A Book You're Not Supposed to Read

Daniel Spulber, ed., *Famous Fables of Economics: Myths and Failures* (Oxford: Blackwell Publishers, 2002).

A collection of peer-reviewed academic journal articles by free-market economists debunking various nirvana fallacy arguments of liberal economists.

Pigou presents a theory that is now taught in every introductory economics book: unregulated markets just about everywhere suffer from what are called positive and negative externalities.[1] The typical example of a negative externality is the pollution that is associated with manufacturing. In unregulated markets, the theory goes, businesses will only consider the cost to themselves of doing business (wages, costs of raw materials, taxes, and so forth), but not the "social costs" in terms of any harm that their pollution might do to other people and property. Therefore, they will produce "too much" to be economically efficient. If they had to incorporate the costs of pollution in their decision-making calculus, then their cost-benefit calculations would lead them to produce less—and therefore to pollute less. Pigou's preferred solution to this problem was for the government to tax every unit of production to make the producers pay for "externalities" such as pollution, assuming that politicians and bureaucrats would be more-or-less omniscient and know what the exact "efficient" level of production was. Anything that is taxed you will get less of, so taxing production would not just reduce production (and employment), but would also reduce pollution, or so the theory goes.

The economics of negative externalities such as pollution will be discussed more fully in the next chapter. But so-called positive externalities are also supposed to be a source of alleged market failure. A positive externality can be thought of as a kind of fringe benefit of the free market. Education, for example, is thought to create positive externalities for society as a whole: a better-educated work force will be more productive, creating more general prosperity; higher levels of education can be a deterrent to crime; education can lead to innovations, discoveries, and technological breakthroughs that benefit all of society; and so on.

But in the eyes of much of the economics profession, this is a Big Problem, not a fringe benefit. The alleged problem is that when people pay for their own education, they pay for their own education. They don't think of the effects of a more prosperous and peaceful society on other people. There will therefore be too little money spent on education, the theory goes. Government must step in and subsidize education for the sake of economic efficiency.

That's the theory, anyway. Pigou himself had great difficulty finding a single example that he could use to illustrate such alleged failures of the free market. Some forty years after his 1912 book *Wealth and Welfare* was published, an ideological fellow traveler (and fellow British economist) named J. E. Meade (who would be awarded the Nobel Prize for Economics in 1977) thought that he had finally discovered the perfect illustration of the problem of market failure caused by the existence of positive externalities. Meade's classic example, which came to be used in myriad economics textbooks, had to do with the case of apple farmers who were in close proximity to beekeepers. As Meade explained:

> Suppose that in a given region there is a certain amount of apple-growing and a certain amount of bee-keeping and that the bees feed on the apple blossom. If the apple farmers apply 10% more labour, land and capital to apple farming, they will increase the output of apples by 10%; but they will also provide more food for the bees. On the other hand, the bee-keepers will not increase the output of honey by 10% by increasing the amount of land, labour and capital to bee-keeping by 10% unless at the same time the apple-farmers also increase their output and so the food of the bees by 10%.... We call this a case of an unpaid factor,

because the situation is due simply and solely to the fact that the apple-farmer cannot charge the beekeeper for the bees' food.[2]

The economic problem, according to J. E. Meade, was that the world would benefit from having 10 percent more honey (which may even make honey a little cheaper as well), but there is no financial incentive for apple orchard owners to increase the food of the bees—apple blossoms—by 10 percent, therefore, the world will have to go without the 10 percent additional honey. Unless, of course, the government steps in and uses taxpayer dollars to subsidize apple orchard owners, which Meade recommended.

Meade wrote that passage in 1952, and it swept the economics textbooks. Then, twenty years later, along came University of Washington economics professor Steven N. S. Cheung, who, as a keen student of the free market, was skeptical of this story of how there were bundles of money (figuratively speaking) to be made in the apple-growing and beekeeping business but orchard owners and beekeepers were just too stupid to realize it and needed to be advised by Cambridge University professors like J. E. Meade who, as far as they knew, had never visited an apple orchard or spoken with a beekeeper.

Steven Cheung did. Living in Washington State, known for its large apple-growing industry, he took it upon himself to do what Cambridge professors apparently almost never do: he left his faculty office and looked around outside to see if there was evidence to support the theories he was supposed to teach in his economics classes. He became quite the expert in the legal and economic aspects of beekeeping and apple orchard management.

In a widely cited article in the *Journal of Law and Economics*, Cheung explained how beekeepers and apple orchard owners in Washington State had in fact, for generations, made contractual[3] agreements for apple orchard owners to pay beekeepers to place their bees in the vicinity of the orchards at pollination time. J. E. Meade's theory was just plain bogus. As Cheung wrote, "Pollination contracts usually include stipulations regarding the number and strength of the colonies, the rental fee per hive, the time of delivery [of the hives to the orchards] and removal of the hives, the protection of the bees from pesticide sprays. . . ."

This is precisely what Meade and Cambridge, Harvard, and other Ivy League economists said could never happen in the free market—but it did. Human beings are problem solvers, especially when there's a financial incentive involved. All it took was a little entrepreneurship on the part of the beekeepers and apple orchard owners, something that is typically absent altogether from the elaborate, hyper-mathematized theories of market failure spun by the J. E. Meades of the world.

> ★ ★ ★
> ## A Tall Tale
> Cheung pointed out in the conclusion of his article that Meade's approach to this issue was even *worse* than the nirvana fallacy—of comparing an ideal or utopia with the actual real world. What Meade had done was "compare the ideal *with a fable*" [emphasis added].[4]

The Fable of the Keys

Leftist economists were quick to update their "market failure" theories to adapt to the information-age economy—by inventing various new theories. One of the more prominent of these was concocted by economist Paul David and colleagues, who claimed that the QWERTY keyboard that is used on almost all computers in the world is actually inferior to a different key configuration, patented in the 1930s, called the Dvorak keyboard.[5] The free market has failed again, said David, by "locking in" an inferior technology. Government should step in and mandate the superior technologies, say the "lock-in" theorists.

The claim that the Dvorak keyboard is superior to the QWERTY keyboard, made by David in the prestigious *American Economic Review* in

A Book You're Not Supposed to Read

Stan Liebowitz and Stephen Margolis, *Winners, Losers, and Microsoft* (Oakland, California: Independent Institute, 2001).

A carefully researched demolition of various theories of "market failure" in the high-tech industries.

1985, near the dawn of the personal computing age, is based on an old report published by the U.S. Navy. It alleged that a keyboard patented by one August Dvorak in 1936 had the advantage of greater speed in typing, less fatigue, and easier learning. For some reason, despite this conclusion based on studies supposedly done by the U.S. Navy, the Dvorak keyboard never caught on.

Economists Stan Liebowitz and Stephen Margolis got hold of the U.S. Navy study and found that it had "many possible biases," all of which "suspiciously, seem to be in favor of the Dvorak design."[6] Hmmm. The Navy report was filled with over-the-top praise for the Dvorak keyboard, comparing it to a jeep (the most popular of all vehicles in the World War II era), while the QWERTY keyboard was compared to an ox—a large, fat, sluggish animal.

Liebowitz and Margolis had uncovered a smoking gun of sorts: it turned out that a Lieutenant Commander August Dvorak was the U.S. Navy's top expert in time-and-motion studies during World War II, and that he had conducted experiments such as the ones mentioned above for the Navy—and "owned the patent on the [Dvorak] keyboard and had received at least $130,000 from the Carnegie Commission for Education for the studies performed."[7]

Apart from this suspicious conflict of interest, Liebowitz and Margolis also reported on a U.S. General Services Administration study of computer keyboards that was done in a much more professional manner and without such obvious conflicts of interests. It concluded that there was no advantage to training typists on the Dvorak keyboard. This study "is ignored in David's history for economists," they wrote.[8] Once again, reality is in conflict with another "model" of market failure.

On top of the claim that the QWERTY keyboard is a "locked-in" market failure, liberal economists claimed that another locked-in market failure had occurred when video cassette recorders became popular: the Betamax brand of videocassette recorder was supposedly superior to its main competitor, the VHS recorder, yet VHS eventually captured the entire market, just like QWERTY did.[9] Your author can remember when the neighborhood Blockbuster video store had two separate sections for video rentals: one for VHS tapes and the other for Betamax tapes. On each visit to the store, it was noticeable that there were fewer and fewer Betamax videos to rent but more and more VHS videos. Eventually there were no Betamax videos at all; VHS had captured the market.

It turns out that the only real "advantage" that the Betamax format had over VHS was that it was first on the market. Numerous studies found that the two machines were essentially the same, with one big exception that turned out to be very important to consumers: the VHS machine had significantly longer recording times, which was the main reason it took away so much of Betamax's market share. King and Queen Consumer had spoken: If the two machines were basically identical and cost the same, but one had longer recording times, then why would anyone buy the other one? The VHS machine was superior in the eyes of millions of consumers—the only opinion that really counts in a free market. Once again, liberal economists were quick to denounce the latest technological development of American capitalism as a "market failure," and once again they were dead wrong.

What Do Politicians Know about Technology, Anyway?

The recommendation of all the liberal economists who, in knee-jerk fashion, have condemned so many technological inventions as "market failures" is more government control and regulation of technology. The result of such policies is perfectly predictable: they will lead to a lobbying free-for-all in which politically savvy businesses will spend millions bribing members of Congress with "campaign contributions" and other favors in return for allowing *their* new technologies onto the market, while blocking their competitors'. More and more money will be spent on this type of lobbying, which is better understood as plunder-seeking, and less and less will be spent on creating new technologies and products for sale. Businesses do not have unlimited funds. Every million dollars spent on plunder-seeking is a million dollars that cannot be spent on research and development of new products and services. Consumers will be the biggest losers from fewer products, fewer technological advances, and higher prices. Instead of technologies and products being chosen by consumers on the basis of which ones serve them best, they will be chosen by politics. King and Queen Consumer will be replaced by members of Congress with the most seniority and committee clout. That will guarantee that myriad inferior technologies *will* be locked in, for once government chooses a product or a technology, it becomes cemented into place indefinitely, protected by layers of special-interest lobbying groups that profit from the government's actions, including government subsidies for the companies that produce the technologies.

Politicians rarely, if ever, admit that they were wrong about anything, and they constantly shift the blame for problems they have caused onto others—particularly those greedy capitalists. It can take many decades for government-supported inferior technologies to be replaced—if they ever are. In the free market, by contrast, no means no. When consumers quit spending their hard-earned dollars on a technology, it's over. They are "hard hearted and callous," as Ludwig von Mises said, and will switch on a dime if a better or cheaper product appears on the market.

Perhaps the most absurd example of how it is not the free market but rather government regulation and control that locks in inferior technologies is the fact that it was not until 2019 that the U.S. government quit using 1970s-era eight-inch floppy discs to operate its nuclear weapons arsenal![10] In addition, congressional hearings in 2016 discovered that the computer system used to track Department of Veterans Affairs benefits was fifty years old and used COBOL, the computer industry "equivalent of Old English." State and local government technology, in general, is just as hopelessly outdated and dysfunctional.[11]

A Book You're Not Supposed to Read

Joseph P. Martino, *Science Funding: Politics and Pork Barrel* (London: Routledge, 1992).

Martino demonstrates how government funding of science results in political or politicized "science" that favors technology that is not the best for society but is sold by politically connected cronies.

Government is a monopoly in nearly everything that it does, and a characteristic of monopolies is that they are not overly concerned about updating their technologies in order to please their customers—in this case, citizens and taxpayers.

Government attempts at "picking winners" with subsidies has long been a carnival of buffoonery. During the 1980s and '90s, liberal economists touted Japan, with its Ministry of International Trade and Investment (MITI), as a model of government-led technology, and urged the U.S. government to do the same. That is, until it became more widely known what MITI had actually been doing: trying to force the Japanese automobile industry to produce only a single "national car"; refusing to give the upstart company Sony the foreign exchange it needed to compete internationally; subsidizing a steel industry that lost some 50,000 jobs in five years; almost destroying its oil refinery industry with price controls, allocation quotas, and other forms of central planning; running a nationalized railroad that was losing $20 million per day; operating one of the least efficient airlines in the world; making its agricultural industry arguably the most heavily subsidized and least efficient in the world; and giving next to no assistance to Japan's most successful industries: automobiles, electronics, and computers.[12]

Another *inherent* feature of government control of technology is corruption. Economist Robert Higgs gives numerous examples in his book *Depression, War, and Cold War*.[13] Take, for example, the history of the A-7 subsonic attack plane once used by the U.S. Navy. As Higgs explains, "By the mid-1970s...Pentagon planners considered it [the A-7] obsolescent. The navy wanted to start acquiring the F/A-18, and the air force, the F-16. In the late 1970s and early 1980s, the air national guard was the only military service that wanted any more A-7s.... Nevertheless, Congress continued to fund the program for years. Why? Because Dallas-based Vought [Corporation], the air national guard, and the powerful Texas congressional delegation demanded it."[14]

Then there's the A-10, a similar type of aircraft. In the late 1970s, the air force decided that it wanted to purchase F-16s instead, but "[t]he large New York delegation [in Congress] and its powerful committee heads—Democrat Joseph Addabbo...and Democrat Samuel Stratton...intervened to stretch out the procurement program."[15]

In the 1960s the Pentagon began requesting to switch from coal to much cheaper oil to heat and fuel its bases in Europe, with an estimated savings of some $20 million per year. The switch was delayed for years because of the clout of one of the most powerful members of Congress, Representative Daniel Flood, who represented coal-producing western Pennsylvania. And on and on it goes, with politics regularly trumping economic rationality, consumer service, and even national defense whenever politics replaces the free market in the allocation of technological resources.

CHAPTER 5

Pollution: Is Capitalism the Cause—or the Cure?

For more than a century, students of economics have been taught that the root cause of pollution and other forms of environmental degradation is the unregulated pursuit of profit in a free market. The theory, which British economist Arthur C. Pigou laid out in his 1912 book *Wealth and Welfare*, goes like this: In pursuit of maximum profits, manufacturers will weigh the benefits to them (revenue) against the costs (wages, material costs, energy bills, taxes, and so forth). But the act of production often involves side effects such as the emission of air pollution from a manufacturing plant. This creates what might be called a "social cost," in the form of harms that may be incurred by people who have nothing to do with the manufacturing or the product: illness from the pollution, unsightliness of nearby neighborhoods, or reduced property values, for example.

According to Pigou and his intellectual descendants—who include virtually all economics textbook authors—private businesses will not take these social costs into account. If they did, the theory goes, their cost-benefit calculations would differ, with higher additional costs leading them to produce—and pollute—less. (Not none, but less.) Thus the root cause of pollution is the unregulated pursuit of profit maximization in a free market with private property and private enterprise. And thus politicians and bureaucrats should be entrusted to solve this problem (along lines prescribed by Arthur C. Pigou, of course).

This is the problem of "*negative* externalities" (the pollution is the negative externality in the example). Government must step in, the theory goes, to either tax or regulate polluting businesses. Pigou even has a tax named after him—the "Pigouvian tax" is a tax on each ton of steel in a steel mill, for example, or on each automobile in an auto plant. Taxes like this deter and diminish production (and cause higher unemployment along the way) to achieve the desired goal of reducing pollution or other social costs of "negative externalities."

According to Pigou, no such problems would exist under socialism since the government authorities, assumed to always act "in the public interest," *would* incorporate social costs into their cost-benefit calculations and produce precisely the efficient amounts of products. As with the case of the positive externalities in the bees–apple orchard example, the negative-externality-from-pollution theory has a certain logic to it. However, reality once again renders this theory of market failure suspect.

Socialist Pollution: The Worst Ever

If the profit motive in a free market is the root cause of pollution, then one would expect that all the countries of the world that *outlawed private enterprise* and the pursuit of profit during the twentieth century—the socialist economies of the Soviet empire, China, and elsewhere—would have had pristine, virtually pollution-free environments. No pursuit of profit by greedy capitalists would mean no pollution. In fact, exactly the opposite happened. The socialist world was (and is) by far the most polluted landscape on earth. Obviously, the pursuit of profit by private enterprise could not have been the cause of this environmental calamity, for the only real private enterprises that existed there were the illegal black markets, and none of them involved large-scale, polluting factories.

In a book on environmental pollution in the Soviet Union, Marshall Goldman wrote that "the attitude that nature is there to be exploited by man is the very essence of the Soviet production ethic."[1] One example Goldman points to is how, in order "to comply with five-year plans for housing and building construction, gravel, sand, and trees around the beaches were used for decades for construction materi-

A Book You're Not Supposed to Read

Murray Feshbach, *Ecocide in the USSR* (New York: Basic Books, 1993).

Feschbach describes the environmental catastrophe that socialism caused in the former Soviet Union.

als. Because there is no private property, this practice caused massive beach erosion which reduced the Black Sea coast by 50 percent between 1920 and 1960."[2] Hotels, hospitals, and a military sanitarium collapsed into the sea, Goldman explained, as the shoreline gave way. There were as many as three hundred landslides per year.

Goldman's book was published in 1972. By the late 1980s, with socialism collapsing in the Soviet empire, journalists were able to get access to these closed totalitarian societies for the first time in many decades, and what they found—and reported on—was an environmental hell. Catastrophic water pollution had killed almost all the fish in the Oka, Volga, Ob, Yenisei, Ural, and Northern Dvina Rivers. Most Soviet factories discharged their waste into the waterways with no pollution controls at all, and mines, oil drilling sites, and ships freely dumped pollutants into any available body of water. Very few cities even had sewer systems by the late 1960s.[3]

It was feared at the time that the Aral Sea could turn into a salt marsh by the year 2000; the Aral and Caspian Seas had been gradually disappearing as large quantities of water were diverted for irrigation. The sturgeon population was so decimated that the Soviets were experimenting with artificial caviar!

Goldman wrote about how hundreds of factories and refineries along the Caspian Sea dumped untreated waste into the sea, a practice that was followed by all major cities. The concentration of pollutants in the Volga River was so great that steamboats were equipped with signs forbidding passengers to throw cigarettes overboard lest the river should catch on fire![4]

Hundreds of millions of gallons of pollution were dumped into Lake Baikal, the largest freshwater lake in the world, for decades, killing off at least half of all animal life there. Giant islands of alkaline sewage, one of which was eighteen miles long and three miles wide, were floating around this great lake.[5]

In socialist Poland, one-third of the population was said to be living in areas of "ecological disaster." In the heavily industrialized Katowice region, the people suffered 15 percent more circulatory disease, 30 percent more tumors, and 47 percent more respiratory disease than in other parts of Poland.[6]

Industrial dust rained down on Polish cities and towns during socialism, depositing cadmium, lead, zinc, and iron. The dust was so heavy that trucks drove through the streets daily spraying water to reduce it. The Vistula River had mercury levels that were twenty-five times higher than what was deemed safe.[7]

In 1990 the new Czech president Vaclav Havel said that Czechoslovakia had "the worst environment in the whole of Europe," with sulfur dioxide levels eight times higher than in the United States and half the forests dead or dying.[8] Similar environmental calamities were discovered in all the other former Soviet "satellite" countries of Europe. Obviously, abolishing private enterprise and criminalizing the legal and peaceful pursuit of profit in a free market not only did not reduce or eliminate environmental degradation, but led to an astronomical increase in it.

Lessons from Socialism's Environmental Nightmares

The environmental nightmares caused by socialism proved that there is more to the problem of pollution than Pigou's fanciful theory of "negative externalities." The problem with socialism is that when all resources are owned by the government, then no one really owns them. There are no property rights other than the claims by politicians to essentially own everything (and everybody). With property rights in a free-market capitalist system, in contrast, people are held legally responsible for the use of their property. At least they will be if there is a reasonably well-functioning government legal system. If they harm others, then they are *liable* for the damage that they cause to others, and that potential liability discourages bad behavior. Under socialism *no one* is held liable when the government denudes forests, pollutes lakes and streams, causes massive illness and death from pollution, and so forth. Whether in democracies or dictatorships, politicians routinely claim "sovereign immunity" to exempt themselves from such responsibility.

When resources are communally owned there is inevitably a "tragedy of the commons."[9] Since no one owns the resources, the incentive is for everyone to get as much as possible out of them as quickly as possible—knowing that everyone else has the same incentive—before they run out. (The depletion of ocean fisheries is a good example of the tragedy of the commons.) The socialist world in the twentieth century was one big commons that tragically caused enormous environmental damage, labeled by some as "ecocide," or ecological suicide.[10]

A Book You're Not Supposed to Read

Terry Anderson and Donald Leal, *Free Market Environmentalism* (New York: Palgrave MacMillan, 2001).

Two of the founding fathers of free-market environmentalism describe how property rights and markets can solve many environmental problems, and why governments so often fail to solve them—or are the cause of the problems in the first place.

In sharp contrast, when people own property, they have strong incentives to take care of it, for if they degrade the property, its value declines, and along with it their private wealth. If they improve the property, then the value will increase, and so will their wealth. This does not guarantee that property owners will never do anything to degrade their own property, but it is certainly the right incentive system to encourage conservation.

This is why the public lakes and streams are so often depleted of fish and full of trash, whereas private farm ponds and lakes in housing developments are much better taken care of. It is why privately-owned homes are generally much better taken care of than government housing "projects." It is why private fishing and hunting clubs conserve fish and wildlife, while the public lakes and streams are over-fished and over-hunted (and plagued by poachers).

A well-functioning legal liability system can protect people from pollution, since damaging another person's health or reducing the value of his property with pollution is a violation of that person's rights, and he can sue for damages. Liability for pollution can be a powerful motivator for businesses to avoid polluting without the need for the heavy hand of government regulators and central planners from the Environmental Protection Agency.

One example of this phenomenon is a notorious waste dump in Upstate New York called Love Canal.[11] The Hooker Chemical Company operated the site in the 1940s and 1950s as a depository of chemical waste. It buried the waste in steel barrels and paved over the site, meeting the federal Environmental Protection Agency's standards by the early 1980s. Then the site was taken over by the local government, which condemned the land under the law of eminent domain and paid Hooker Chemical Company $1 for it. The company warned the local politicians about the need to contain the chemicals in the site, but they ignored the warning, built a school on the site, removed the protective cap on top of the site, and sold some of the land to a developer without disclosing the hazard. This allowed toxic waste to escape into the ground water—a disaster for which the local politicians were solely responsible. They denied responsibility and lied about it, blaming the chemical company. In any case, as politicians, they were not financially liable for the damages they had caused to the community.

The chemical company was meticulously careful because it knew that it would be liable for any such damages. The politicians behaved in the opposite manner in full knowledge that they would *not* be liable. This was not "socialism," but it was an example of *socializing* a relatively small piece of property, and the results were very harmful to the environment of Upstate New York and to the residents there. The root cause of the problem was *political control* of resources. When the profit-seeking Hooker Chemical Company owned the land, the realities of liability forced it to behave responsibly, unlike local politicians.

This doesn't mean that Pigou's analysis is completely wrong, however. When governments fail to perform their basic duties, such as enforcing legal liability for the harm one person (or business) imposes on others, as they often do, then polluters are more likely to get away with pollution. In fact, in his renowned book *The Transformation of American Law*, Harvard University legal scholar Professor Morton J. Horwitz documented how collectivist ideology infected legal thinking in the nineteenth century, leading to the purposeful abrogation of governmental responsibilities regarding liability law.[12]

In particular, economic development came to be deemed a primary objective of government at all levels, and this affected the legal system. The collectivist notion that no individual or group of individuals should be allowed to stand in the way of economic progress for the whole society took hold. So when a factory opened up and employed, say, hundreds of people but polluted the local air and water, the relatively small number of people negatively affected by the pollution should not stand in the way of economic progress of the majority—or so the reasoning went. In case after case, year after year, decisions were made to let polluters off the hook according to some version of this collectivist reasoning, wrote Horwitz. So by the early twentieth century, Pigou's era, there were in fact a great many factories that were pursuing profits in markets that were lightly regulated but, more important, often void of enforcement of strict liability law. The government's legal system, not free-market competition, was the main problem.

Free-Market Competition *Conserves* Resources

Students who take an introductory course in economics are taught that businesses strive to maximize their profits, sometimes succeeding and most of the time failing! They are also taught that the flip side or mirror image of "profit maximizing" is cost minimization. Profit, from an accounting point of view, is simply the difference between sales revenue taken in and costs incurred to produce and market a product or service. There are three ways to increase the amount of profit by competing: 1) increase sales and sales revenue, 2) decrease costs, or 3) both of the above. Students are typically taught about various techniques that businesses can use to minimize their costs and therefore maximize their profits. Your author taught university economics for forty-one years, and during that time students rarely made the connection that "minimizing costs" includes conserving or minimizing the amount of natural (and other) resources used to produce products or services. In other words, the process of competition itself—and indeed, the pursuit of profit—encourages resource conservation.

A favorite anecdote of your author is a lecture by an old friend named Harry Teasley, who was the CEO of the Coca-Cola Nestle company. In a Rotary Club–style speech that he gave many times, he described the decision-making process at Coca-Cola that led to a dramatic decline in the use of aluminum in soda cans (by 80 percent or so, if memory serves). Coca-Cola was not motivated by environmentalist ideology, he explained, or a newfound sense of responsibility to "society," but by the responsibility to make as much money as possible for Coca-Cola shareholders (their "fiduciary responsibility").

When Coca-Cola engineers figured out how to use so much less aluminum in soda cans, they must have cut the cost of doing business by many millions of dollars annually. Harry Teasley described this piece of American business history with a story about how, when he was in a college fraternity, a "rite of passage" among the fraternity brothers was to (stupidly) crush a Coke can on one's forehead, as in the famous scene in the movie *Animal House* where John Belushi performed that stunt. Today, he said, his ten-year-old granddaughter can rip a Coke can apart with her bare hands because it uses so little aluminum and is so thin. The truth is just the opposite of the story told over a century ago by Arthur C. Pigou: free-market competition drives conservation. And it is government bureaucracy that is wasteful and irresponsible as a general rule, for bureaucrats pay no personal price for being wasteful with other people's resources and are not rewarded for taking good care of them either. They get paid the same no matter what their performance is like.

Like many other corporations, Coca-Cola recycles when it is profitable to do so. Another memorable story from that speech Harry Teasley gave was how, with its Hi-C Orange Juice business, the company was left with mountains of orange peels that it sent to landfills or gave away to hog farmers. Until, that is, a Coca-Cola chemist figured out how to use the orange peels to make perfume, a new side business for the company. There's nothing objectionable per se about recycling, as long as it's profitable, Teasley said. Thus there's not always a need to pressure, ostracize, or coerce people into doing it.

So-called environmentalists who refuse to acknowledge that property rights and markets can solve many environmental problems, or that socialism has led to so many awful environmental catastrophes in the world, reveal that they are not really concerned about conservation after all. They have been appropriately labeled "watermelons"—green on the outside, but red on the inside—because their real objective is to destroy capitalism and replace it with socialism.

CHAPTER 6

The "Free-Rider" Fallacy

Since at least the time of Adam Smith (the late eighteenth century), the argument has been made that there are certain types of goods or services that are unique in that, even though everyone supposedly benefits from them, some people will not voluntarily pay for them, leading to an inadequate supply for the whole of society. These goods are labeled "public goods," and their unique characteristics are that, once they are provided, they are "nonrival" and "nonexcludable." Take, for example, mosquito abatement, something that many local governments are involved in. Given that mosquitoes are more than just an annoyance—they can also spread deadly diseases—their abatement by spraying poisons on land, water, and in the air is said to be a "public good." That is, the fact that you benefit from disease reduction does not mean that your neighbors do not. With a private good such as a can of soda, in contrast, if one person consumes it then by definition no one else does. It is "rival in consumption," to use the clunky language of economics.

It would be impossible, the theory goes, to exclude the people who aren't willing to pay from the reduced incidence of disease caused by mosquito abatement. Once the benefit has been created, how could you? Order people

★ ★ ★
Taken for a Ride

Taxes are not voluntary. People have had their homes confiscated for not paying even small property tax bills, and failure to pay income tax can put you in prison for quite a few years. The average jail time for income tax evasion in the United States is three to five years, with a fine of up to $250,000.[1] In 2019 an eighty-three-year-old Michigan man had his house seized by the Oakland County government and sold at auction after he miscalculated and underpaid his property tax by $8.41. He lost his house, and the government bureaucracy kept the profit from the sale.[2]

to remain inside so as not to benefit from the mosquito abatement?

This means that for this type of "public good" there will always be some people who will have a "let George do it" attitude. They are the supposed "free riders." Their thinking is that, since mosquito abatement (and all other public goods) are valued by some, *those* people will contribute or volunteer to pay for it so that "I don't have to." In small groups such as a family or a relatively small neighborhood, it is common for everyone to chip in to provide communal benefits. The problem is when the numbers increase. In the city-wide mosquito abatement scenario, it is not hard to imagine that not every adult in a town of, say, fifty to a hundred thousand people will voluntarily contribute if asked. In fact, it is not unlikely that *most* would choose to free ride on the contributions of others.

Thus, virtually every university economics student in the world is taught, people are starving for more and more government, whether they know it or not, but they must be forced to pay for it. In order to avoid this crisis, government must step in with its usual tools of threats, intimidation, and imprisonment to force everyone to pay for its public goods. Or so the theory goes. The solution to the free-rider problem is to use the coercive powers of the state to force people to pay for the so-called public goods through taxation—to turn free riders into *forced* contributors—even those who have no use at all for whatever "public" good the state wants to produce.

As prominent (and predominant) as it is in the economics textbooks, there are a lot of problems with this theory. For one thing, hardly any kind of good or service is truly a net benefit to "the public"—to *everyone* in society. "National defense" is often used as an example of a public good in the textbooks, but it is important to note that even the declaration of war on Japan after Pearl Harbor did not have unanimous approval in the U.S. House of Representatives, let alone among the entire population. And of course foreign policy, which determines which wars are to be fought and how, is enormously contentious and never has the unanimous approval of the entire public.

Many members of the public consider various wars to be unjust and therefore public "bads," not goods. Even our mosquito abatement example, which has also been used in textbooks, is viewed by many as a public *bad*. In your author's town the county government has a policy of using low-flying aircraft at dawn to spray wetlands with mosquito and mosquito larvae–killing chemicals. Quite a few people in the town are upset and even outraged by this practice, which they consider to be a public bad from an environmental perspective—and from a health perspective. They believe that their health is being harmed by the chemicals that are being spread in the name of improving public health! In other words, the whole concept of a "public good" is dubious.

Another problem with the theory of the "free-rider problem" is that there are examples all around us of private individuals and groups providing myriad types of goods and services that are "nonrival" and "nonexcludable." Americans are probably the most charitable people in the world, as measured by charitable contributions for everything from medical research on cancer and other diseases to animal protection, neighborhood beautification, free concerts, and thousands of other things. The very existence of so many privately funded charities proves that the free-rider problem is not nearly as severe a problem as students of economics are led to believe.

In 2009, political scientist Elinor Ostrom became the first woman to be awarded the Nobel Memorial Prize in Economics, for her lifelong work

demonstrating how people all over the world have voluntarily devised ways of providing all kinds of public goods without governmental compulsion of any kind.[3] There is even a history of private currencies that existed before governments monopolized the monetary systems of the world with their "central banks." There is also a history of private streets and roads. Columbia, Maryland, and Reston, Virginia, are two towns whose entire infrastructure of roads was built by private developers, despite the fact that roads have been defined as public goods and therefore the province of government since the time of the American founding.[4]

A case can be made that the rule of law, government protection of property rights, limited constitutional government, and a free-market economy benefit just about everyone, but generations ago such things became only a small proportion of what governments actually do.[5] At the federal level, the overwhelming majority of government programs are income-transfer programs that benefit one segment of the public at the expense of another and have nothing to do with public goods or free-rider problems. Many members of the public believe that welfare spending, although it benefits some—especially the well-paid government bureaucrats who administer the system—also creates public bads by creating negative work incentives and getting fathers off the hook for abandoning their children, among other things.[6]

Especially at the state and local levels of government, it is hard to think of any service provided by governments that is not also provided by private businesses (or private nonprofit organizations), usually at a fraction of the cost and with higher quality and customer service to boot. There are thousands of private schools and hospitals that compete with government schools and hospitals. There are volunteer fire departments and thousands of private security guards. Economist Bruce Benson pointed out that there are more private police in the United States than there are government police.[7]

Two Centuries of the Free-Rider Fallacy

Politicians have been making free-rider-style arguments for taxpayer funding of things like roads and canals since the early days of America, long before there was any such thing as an economics profession. The most prominent among them was Alexander Hamilton, the first U.S. treasury secretary. In his 1791 *Report on Manufactures*, Hamilton argued that private investment would not be sufficient to adequately support road and canal building, projects that were labeled "internal improvements" at the time.[8] (Today—after two centuries of experience—they have acquired names with more negative connotations: "corporate welfare," "crony capitalism," or "pork-barrel politics"). President Thomas Jefferson's treasury secretary, Albert Gallatin, proposed a ten-year taxpayer-funded road- and canal-building project known as the Gallatin Plan. The plan went nowhere, however, because Jefferson himself believed that the Constitution would have to be amended to allow for the expenditure of taxpayer funds on such things, since they were not among the delegated powers enumerated in Article 1, Section 8, of the Constitution.[9]

Jefferson's successor, President James Madison, vetoed an "internal improvements" bill on his very last day in office. The legislation was sponsored by Congressman Henry Clay, the owner of a large hemp-growing slave plantation in Kentucky who wanted the taxpayers to foot the bill for delivering his hemp to market. President Madison, the "father of the Constitution," believed that it was time to teach the nation a lesson in constitutionalism. Reiterating Jefferson's argument, he pointed out that giving taxpayers' money to corporations to build roads and canals was not among the enumerated powers of the federal government, and vetoed the legislation.[10]

During the 1830s President Andrew Jackson vetoed several "internal improvement" bills, denouncing them in his farewell address as "this plan of unconstitutional expenditure for the purpose of corrupt influence."[11]

While all of this was going on, private investors, entrepreneurs, and American communities were busy disproving the Hamilton-Clay free-rider rationale for taxpayer funding of roads and canals by building thousands of miles of privately funded roads and canals. As economist Daniel Klein wrote in a peer-reviewed academic journal on the subject, as early as 1800 there were sixty-nine private road-building companies in America.[12] In the next three decades, writes Klein:

> [T]he movement built new roads at rates previously unheard of in America. Over $11 million was invested in turnpikes in New York, some $6.5 million in New England, and over $4.5 million in Pennsylvania.... Between 1794 and 1840, 238 private New England turnpike companies built and operated about 3,750 miles of road. New York led all other states in turnpike mileage with over 4,000 as of 1821. Pennsylvania was second, reaching a peak of about 2,400 miles in 1832. New Jersey companies operated 500 miles by 1821.... Between 1810 and 1845 over 400 [private] turnpikes were chartered and built.[13]

Daniel Klein explains how "market failure" theorists, in their zeal to denounce economic freedom and entrepreneurship and advocate government interventionism, have the bad habit of studiously ignoring reality. He discovered that, while the turnpike companies of the early nineteenth century could only offer investors a 3 percent return on their investments, lower than many other investments, local merchants understood that the roads built with their investments would bring more commerce to their towns and enrich just about everyone there as a result.

It was also understood that investments in roads would increase the size of local markets. It would take a while, but in the end the real return would be a lot more than that 3 percent. Businesspeople in larger cities even invested in the turnpike companies because they understood that that would help them sell *their* products in the hinterlands. Some states, such as Connecticut, exempted income earned from turnpike company stock from taxation.[14]

A Book You're Not Supposed to Read

David Beito, Peter Gordon, and Alex Tabarrok, eds., *The Voluntary City* (Oakland, California: Independent Institute, 2009).

Discusses the superior private provision of just about all services that governments also provide.

Klein also writes how the "spirit of voluntary association" that was so pervasive in early America also played a part. Town meetings and local newspapers urged everyone to invest to overcome any free riding. The turnpike companies also ingeniously offered shares of stock in return for rights of way over private property, as a sort of privatized "law" of eminent domain.

Some state governments did get into the "internal improvement" subsidy game during the 1830s and 1840s—and it was a financial catastrophe in state after state. A young Abraham Lincoln, as a leader of the Whig party in the Illinois legislature in the mid-1830s, procured some $11 million for the building of roads and canals. It turned out to be a colossal disaster of fraud, mismanagement, and corruption. As William Herndon, Lincoln's personal secretary while president, would write, "[T]he stupendous operations of the scheme dazzled the eyes of nearly everybody, but in the end it rolled up a debt so enormous as to impede the otherwise marvelous progress of Illinois. The burdens imposed by this Legislature...became so monumental in size...that...the monster of [debt] repudiation showed its hideous face above the waves of popular indignation."[15]

Because politicians have no personal stake invested in such projects, they are invariably sloppy or corrupt, or both, in how they manage them. If the projects succeed, they gladly take the credit, but if they do not succeed, it's no skin off their backs (or pennies from their bank accounts). Thus in state after state during the pre–Civil War era the results were the same: waste, fraud, corruption, theft of government funds, and little, if anything, built with all those millions. It was such a debacle that by the time of the Civil War, all states except for Massachusetts and Missouri had amended their constitutions to prohibit the use of taxpayer funds to subsidize "internal improvements." And Missouri got around to doing the same in 1875.[16]

After the Civil War, the government-subsidized transcontinental railroads repeated the financial disasters that the states had experienced with "internal improvements," but on a much grander scale. So much so that one is inclined to think such corruption is the main purpose of such schemes. There is so much money to be pocketed by the politically connected, even if the public in general sees little or no benefit. The Crédit Mobilier scandal that was associated with the government-subsidized Central Pacific and Union Pacific Railroads was the biggest corruption scandal in U.S. history up to that point. It was also the biggest political patronage handout scheme in history; it created fortunes for dozens of politically connected business owners.

At around the same time, and in sharp contrast to the criminality, corruption, wastefulness, and mismanagement of the government-subsidized transcontinental railroads, the entrepreneur James J. Hill built the Great Northern transcontinental railroad line without a dime of government subsidy, not even the land grants that his competitors enjoyed. It was by far the most efficiently built and operated transcontinental railroad of the day.

And it is another nail in the coffin of "free-rider" thinking, according to which only government-subsidized transcontinental railroads could exist.[17]

But, But... What about Lighthouses?!

In the tradition of government interventionists who ignore history and reality when it conflicts with their theories condemning economic freedom and entrepreneurship are the numerous economic writers who have cited the building of lighthouses as their go-to example of the supposedly inherent failures of the free market due to the free-rider problem.

The famous nineteenth-century British philosopher John Stuart Mill wrote that "it is a proper office of government to build and maintain lighthouses...since it is impossible that the ships at sea which are benefited by a lighthouse, should be made to pay a toll...no one would build lighthouses from motives of personal interest, unless indemnified and rewarded from a compulsory levy made by the state."[18]

In his 1901 textbook *The Principles of Political Economy*, the influential British philosopher and economist Henry Sidgwick wrote that the operators of lighthouses would be "practically incapable" of charging a fee for the benefits of a lighthouse so that the light "must be largely enjoyed by ships on which no toll could be conveniently imposed."[19] Arthur C. Pigou himself would repeat Sidgwick's theory in his own writings.

Mill, Sidgwick, and Pigou were very influential within the economics profession of their day, so much so that successive generations of textbook writers would highlight lighthouses as *their* example of a service that *had* to be financed by taxpayers and administered by government bureaucrats to avoid the free-rider problem. In his famous *Economics* textbook Paul Samuelson wrote of certain "public services" without which "community life would be unthinkable," and listed lighthouses among these services. Lighthouses save lives and cargoes, he wrote, but "lighthouse keepers cannot reach out to collect fees from skippers.... Philosophers and statesmen have always recognized the necessary role of government in such cases" because "a businessman could not build it for a profit. . . ."[20]

About a decade after Paul Samuelson wrote those words in the sixth edition of his textbook, Nobel laureate economist Ronald Coase did something that Mill, Sidgwick, Pigou, and Samuelson had apparently not thought of: he actually researched and studied the operations of the real-world lighthouse industry. What he found was that as early as the seventeenth century the British government had claimed monopoly power over lighthouse-building, but was motivated to build hardly any lighthouses. In the period from 1610 to 1675, Coase wrote, no lighthouses were built by the British government despite the growing demand for them by shippers.[21] So the private sector stepped in to respond to this governmental failure and built at least ten lighthouses during that period. Note that this is exactly *the opposite* of the standard theory of market failure with regard to lighthouses: the historical reality is that it was *government* that failed to provide the benefits of lighthouses, and private entrepreneurs who did provide them. Not only that, but Coase found that the British government even attempted to protect its monopoly authority by opposing the efforts of private individuals to build lighthouses (although without success).[22] The fact, Coase found, was that those who purported to be "motivated by a sense of public service did not build the lighthouses," and "the primary motive" of those who did build them was "personal gain."[23] Once again, government fails and markets work.

Collecting tolls from shippers was not hard at all, contrary to the dire warnings of Mill, Samuelson, and other "market failure" theorists. As Coase explained, "The tolls were collected at the ports by agents...varying with the size of the vessel.... It was normally a rate per ton for each voyage."[24]

Private entrepreneurs built and operated British lighthouses for almost a century and a half before the British government decided that they were such a good tax revenue source that it banned further private operations and monopolized the practice. No doubt the government proceeded to operate them, as the saying goes, with all the efficiency of the Department of Motor Vehicles and the compassion of the Internal Revenue Service.

In other words, generations of economics students were miseducated about the free-rider problem with the vaunted lighthouse example that pervaded the textbooks. As Coase concluded in 1974, until he came along "no economist, to my knowledge, has ever made a comprehensive study of lighthouse finance and administration. The lighthouse is simply plucked out of the air to serve as an illustration."[25] ("Straw man" would be a more accurate label than "illustration.")

The odd thing about stories such as this is that while the "market failure" theorists condemn the greed of profit-seeking businesses, they refuse to study or acknowledge how that same profit-seeking motive solves so many of the imaginary problems that they incessantly invent in their prolific writings about the supposed failures of economic freedom and free enterprise. And in their boundless faith in the curative features of governmental coercion, taxation, and bureaucracy, they fail to notice how greed and personal ambition can motivate bureaucrats and elected officials, too.

CHAPTER 7

Un-Natural Monopolies

Every university economics student is taught that government must own and operate, or at least heavily regulate, "public utilities" such as electricity, water supply, natural gas, telephone services, and other "necessities." Supposedly, it was determined during the early twentieth century that large-scale mass production led to the benefits of economies of scale—declining per-unit costs as production expanded—but there was also a cost: one large corporation that achieved economies of scale would be able to underprice all other competitors and drive them from the market, creating a "natural monopoly." (This is essentially a version of the discredited theory of "predatory pricing.")

Therefore, the theory goes, government must step in and either take over the public utility industry or regulate its prices (and other business practices) in order to prevent monopoly. It is assumed that the politicians and government bureaucrats who then control the operations and pricing of the public utility industries will do so in the "public interest." Governments should therefore create what are called "franchise monopolies," whereby ostensibly privately owned companies are granted monopolies and their prices are regulated by government to (in theory) prevent high monopolistic prices for these "necessities." It is assumed that government-owned public utility industries will set prices "in the public interest." This is yet another version of the free-market-run-amok-and-politicians-on-white-horses-to-the-rescue theory of "market failure."

And like so many other theories of "market failure," it is dead wrong. Despite more than a century of storytelling about "natural monopoly" in the economics textbooks, there is in fact no evidence at all that during the late nineteenth and early twentieth centuries there existed any such thing as "natural" utility monopolies created in the way described by the theory. Professor Harold Demsetz of UCLA researched the topic and found:

> Six electric light companies were organized in the one year of 1887 in New York City. Forty-five electric light enterprises had the legal right to operate in Chicago in 1907. Prior to 1895, Duluth, Minnesota, was served by five electric lighting companies, and Scranton, Pennsylvania, had four in 1906.... During the latter part of the 19th century, competition was the usual situation in the gas industry in this country. Before 1884, six competing companies were operating in New York City...competition was common and especially persistent in the telephone industry...Baltimore, Chicago, Cleveland, Columbus, Detroit, Kansas City, Minneapolis, Philadelphia, Pittsburgh, and St. Louis, among the larger cities, had at least two telephone services in 1905.[1]

In an extreme understatement, Professor Demsetz concluded that "one begins to doubt that scale economies characterized the utility industry at the time when regulation replaced market competition."[2] Governments did create monopolies everywhere in the public utilities industries during the early twentieth century with their "franchise monopolies"—but there was nothing "natural" about it. Monopolizing this large and important segment of the American economy had nothing to do with protecting the public from monopoly pricing by phantom "natural" free-market monopolies.

Even if a private utility corporation had managed to become a *temporary* monopoly, that would still have been better than the *government-protected utilities monopolies* established by state and local governments all over America in the twentieth century. The fact is, in the absence of government protection, private monopolies are always temporary and fleeting; there's just too much money to be made by potential competitors.

★ ★ ★
Some Monopolies Are More Equal than Others

Nobel laureate economist F. A. Hayek explained, "Private monopoly is scarcely ever complete and even more rarely of long duration or able to disregard potential competition. But a state monopoly is always a state-protected monopoly—protected against both potential competition and effective criticism."[3]

The True Origins of Public Utility Monopolies

Much of the theory of "natural monopoly" was due to the work of economist Richard T. Ely, a cofounder of the American Economic Association (1885) and a leader of the early twentieth-century Progressive movement who was a professor at Johns Hopkins University in Baltimore. Ely's research on the Gas Light Company of Baltimore figures prominently in the history of the natural monopoly theory.

Ely's writings were incorporated into a book entitled *The Gas Light Company of Baltimore* by economist George T. Brown, published by the Johns Hopkins University Press in 1936.[4] Brown chronicled how the Baltimore utilities company had struggled to compete with more and more new competitors in the gas light business (before electricity) for decades, resorting to lobbying the state legislature to deny corporate charters to new competitors. (After Thomas Edison invented the means of commercializing electricity, all the gas light companies became gas light and electricity companies.) When monopoly did finally appear in Baltimore (and elsewhere) in the electric power industry, it was because of government intervention, not free-market competition and economies of scale.

Brown writes about how a bill was introduced into the Maryland state assembly in 1890 that "called for an annual payment to the city [of Baltimore] from the Consolidated Gas Company of $10,000 a year and 3 percent of all dividends declared in return for the privilege of enjoying a 25-year monopoly."[5] This tactic was then replicated in American city after city. It was an unholy, corrupt alliance between corporations and governments to establish monopolies and then share the monopoly loot with the governments that created the monopolies. It was a veiled form of taxation, in other words, and had nothing whatsoever to do with economies of scale or the theories of Richard T. Ely.

Not all economists were bamboozled by Ely's theories and the government-protected monopolies they helped to put in place. University of Illinois economist Horace M. Gray wrote in a peer-reviewed academic journal article that "between 1907 and 1938, the policy of state-protected monopoly became firmly established over a significant portion of the economy and became the keystone of modern public utility regulation.... [T]he public utility status was to be the haven of refuge for all aspiring monopolists who found it too difficult, too costly, or too precarious to secure and maintain monopoly by private action alone."[6]

Gray entertainingly pointed out how virtually every "aspiring monopolist" in the country had adopted the habit of begging governments to be labeled a "public utility," including the radio, real estate, milk, airline, coal, oil, and agricultural industries, among many others. He concluded by condemning the "natural monopoly" theory as a "confused rationalization" for "the sinister forces of private privilege and monopoly."[7] And he was exactly right.

The effect of the government-protected monopolies in the public utilities industries was the opposite of what the "natural monopoly" theorists predicted: government electric utility rate–fixing commissioners were quickly captured by industry lobbyists. Economist Gregg Jarrell found that in twenty-five states that instituted state electric utility regulation between 1912 and 1917, the effect was to *raise prices* by 46 percent and profits by 38 percent while *reducing* the level of service provided by 23 percent—just as any standard economic theory of monopoly would predict.[8]

Another University of Illinois economist, Professor Walter J. Primeaux, devoted much of his career to researching the electric utility industries. He discovered that there are several dozen American cities that never did rely on the Ely theory of "natural monopoly" to justify state-protected monopolies in that industry. Instead, they allowed direct competition by multiple companies. Not geographic market sharing within a city but direct, head-to-head competition throughout the entire city. In his book *Direct Electric Utility Competition: The Natural Monopoly Myth*, Primeaux found that in those American cities the results were vigorous price competition compared to franchise-monopoly cities; better customer service; *lower* costs and prices, contrary to natural monopoly theory; and no serious "price wars." Consumers, he discovered, themselves prefer competition to government-protected monopoly. What a surprise![9] Similar results were found in studies of the cable television[10] and telephone[11] industries.

The Politicians-on-White-Horses Theory of Antitrust Regulation

Another statist fable that all university economics students are taught is that yet another wheel fell off of American capitalism in the late nineteenth

A Book You're Not Supposed to Read

Dominick Armentano, *Antitrust: The Case for Repeal* (Auburn, Alabama: Mises Institute, 2020).

Based on his careful study of fifty-five of the most famous federal antitrust cases, the author makes the case that antitrust has always been a protectionist, anti-competitive racket and should be abolished.

century in the form of "merger waves" that created rampant monopoly of industries. Many of the corporations involved were called "trusts" at the time, so the U.S. government came to the rescue, like a hero on a white horse riding in to save the day with an "antitrust" law. The 1890 law was called the Sherman Antitrust Act after Ohio senator John Sherman, the brother of the famous Civil War general William Tecumseh Sherman and chairman of the Senate finance committee at the time.[12] It vaguely outlawed conspiracies "in restraint of trade."

While it is true that there was a merger wave in the late 1880s, it is unequivocally *not* true that the merger wave lessened competition and caused prices to rise. Precisely the opposite is true: mergers were *a form of competition*. As was widely known by economists—but ignored by too many politicians—the effect of the mergers was a *drop* in prices, the opposite of what "rampant monopolization" would do. In fact, the period from the end of the Civil War in 1865 to the turn of the century was a period of overall price *deflation* in the United States thanks to the burgeoning industrial revolution with its mass production, invention of myriad new industries and products, and, yes, corporate mergers.[13]

The American Economic Association, which as we have seen was created in 1885, was new at the time, and there were only a few dozen people in the entire country who held positions as professors of economics. Among them, there was near unanimous agreement that the Sherman Antitrust Act would *impede* competition and should therefore not be enacted.[14] Richard T. Ely himself wrote that "large scale production is a thing by which no means necessarily signifies monopolized production."[15] There was general agreement within the economics profession of the time that large-scale production produced competitive benefits to consumers through economies of scale.[16] The overwhelming consensus was that suppressing mergers and large-scale production would cause *less* competition and *higher* prices for consumers. But the economists' views were studiously ignored by Senator Sherman and most of his congressional colleagues because they did not support their agenda of instituting more government control and central planning of the U.S. economy with antitrust legislation.

★ ★ ★

Why Did the Professional Economists Go Along with the Antitrust Myth?

The late Nobel laureate George Stigler of the University of Chicago once remarked that economists eventually came to support antitrust laws because they learned that they could earn "more than the minimum wage" as antitrust consultants to corporations and governments.[17]

The Sherman Antitrust Act soon became a major plank of the political platform of the Progressive movement in America. The fable of Senator John Sherman riding into Washington, D.C., on a white horse (figuratively speaking) to save America from rapacious monopolists was spread far and wide, especially in the economics textbooks used in business schools and law schools in the increasingly government-funded and -controlled education system during the twentieth century. For some ninety years this fable was challenged by precious few economists.

Yours truly smelled a big fat rat while researching this topic in the 1980s and conducted a survey of the Congressional Record of 1889 and 1890 to determine which industries, exactly, were being accused of monopolization by the supporters of the Sherman Antitrust Act.[18] The standard theory of monopoly within the mainstream of the economics profession is that monopolies increase prices and reduce production levels compared to competitive industries. So I gathered historical economic data on prices and production for seventeen of the industries accused of monopolization during the congressional debates over the Sherman Act. Surprisingly, no other economist had apparently ever done this! What I found was that while real (inflation-adjusted) gross domestic product (GDP) increased by about 24 percent from 1880 to 1890, the industries accused of "restricting output" increased their production by 175 percent on average, seven times more than the economy in general. For example, steel production rose by 258 percent, zinc 156 percent, coal 153 percent, steel rails 142 percent, petroleum 79 percent, and sugar 75 percent.[19] And during that same time period, as the consumer price index (CPI) fell by 7 percent, the "trusts" that were accused of monopolization dropped their prices by far more. The price of steel rail fell by 53 percent, refined sugar became 22 percent cheaper, lead declined in price by 12 percent, and zinc by 20 percent, for example. This trend of production in these industries dominated by "trusts"—the supposed "natural monopolies"—outstripping GDP as a whole and prices declining faster in these industries than the CPI continued on for the next decade as well.[20]

In reality, the late nineteenth-century "trusts" were the most dynamic, entrepreneurial, innovative, expanding industries in America, creating hundreds of thousands of jobs and inventing myriad new products. Such dynamism always puts other, less innovative businesses in the position of having to do one of two things: 1) compete, or 2) lobby the government to outlaw or hinder their more innovative, price-cutting and production-expanding rivals. Choice #2 was the impetus for the Sherman Antitrust Act (and almost all successive antitrust regulation).

The *New York Times*, which had originally supported the Sherman Act, reversed its editorial stance after observing the antics of Senator Sherman and his fellow Republicans. It turns out that Sherman was also the sponsor of the October 1, 1890, McKinley Tariff, which increased the average duty on imports to about 50 percent. The Sherman Act was enacted into law in

June of 1890. (President William McKinley was such a protectionist that he was called "The Napoleon of Protectionism").

At the time, everyone knew that protectionist tariffs were a tool of monopolists since they shielded domestic manufacturers from international competition, allowing them to raise their prices (and often to allow the quality of their products to decline because of the lessened competitive pressures). In other words, the real source of monopoly in 1890 was the protectionist tariff sponsored by Senator John Sherman, not the "antitrust" law sponsored by Senator John Sherman. Thus the *New York Times* editorialized on October 1, 1890: "That so-called Anti-Trust law was passed to deceive the people and to clear the way for the enactment of this ... law relating to the tariff. It was projected in order that the [Republican] party organs might say to the opponents of tariff extortion and protected combinations, 'Behold! We have attacked the Trusts. The Republican party is the enemy of all such rings.'"[21]

The *New York Times* even pointed out that Senator Sherman had criticized the "trusts" for "subverting the tariff system" of high prices with all of their price-cutting, competition, and low prices. That must be stopped, Sherman had said, and according to the *Times* that was the purpose of his law, which the *Times* referred to as the "Campaign Contributors Tariff Bill," since the real authors of the bill were the corporations that had lavishly funded the Republican Party. (Until about the turn of the century, the Democratic Party was the party of free trade and the Republican Party was the party of government interventionism. That changed beginning with the 1896 election, when the "Progressives" took over the Democratic Party.)

CHAPTER 8

Asymmetric (Backwards) Economics

It seems as though the economics profession will never give up on the nirvana fallacy. It has gotten so out of hand that Nobel Prizes have been given to people who claim that the division of labor—the economic glue that holds human civilization together, as we saw in chapter 1—is itself an example of "market failure"! Economists Joseph Stiglitz, George Akerlof, and Michael Spence were awarded the Nobel Prize in Economics by the Swedish central bank in 2001 for their writings on what they called "asymmetric information," which is their preferred phrase for the *division of knowledge* in society.

The "division of labor" language goes all the way back to Adam Smith's famous 1776 book *The Wealth of Nations* (if not further), and it has a prominent place in all economics textbooks to this day. The language made perfect sense all throughout the "machine age," when brawn rather than brain dominated labor markets. In today's information-age economy a more appropriate phrase would be "division of knowledge," since so many industries are knowledge-based, as opposed to being strictly rooted in assembly line manufacturing of steel, cars, textiles, and so forth.

The benefits to society of the division of knowledge are the same as with the division of labor. The electrical engineers who have designed and redesigned your cell phone are specialists in that endeavor, and you are not. You are a specialist in *your* job or *your* field of specialization. You earn money doing what you do and then you enjoy the benefits of having the internet at your fingertips all day long (among other things) by purchasing their cell phone products.

The "asymmetric information" theorists seem never to have learned this basic Econ 101 lesson even though some of them are Nobel Prize winners! Their main claim is that because the producers and sellers of products know more about their products than their customers do, they can easily swindle their customers by selling them "lemons"—a term that signifies defective or fraudulent services.

George Akerlof (the husband of Janet Yellen, who has served as U.S. treasury secretary, chair of the Federal Reserve Board, and chair of President Clinton's Council of Economic Advisors) introduced this theory in a 1970 article in the *Quarterly Journal of Economics* about the used-car market.[1] Because the sellers of used cars know more about the cars than the buyers do, he argued, they will be able to sell many a "lemon" for the same price as a good-quality car. This would cause the used-car market to be dominated by lower and lower quality cars and maybe eventually disappear altogether, Akerlof predicted, since consumers would eventually get sick of all the "lemons."

Akerlof's article was flatly contradicted by reality on the day that it was published. Thirty-day product warrantees, which existed in 1970, were the used-car industry's way of eliminating customer concerns about "lemons." Thirty days is plenty of time to determine whether your new car is a lemon. The used-car warranty market has expanded greatly since then, with companies such as CarMax offering seven-day, no-questions-asked return policies on all the cars that it sells and also selling much longer extended warranties to customers who want them. The free market had solved the "lemons problem" before Akerlof invented it, and it continues to provide new ways to protect consumers against the supposed perils of "asymmetric information."

In addition to misunderstanding the meaning of the division of labor and knowledge in society, the "asymmetric information" theorists also misunderstand how competition works. If a used-car dealer (or any other businessperson) is known to be dishonest, he creates a profit opportunity for his competitors armed with superior warranties and business reputations. In a competitive market, the more honest car dealers will take market share away from the more dishonest ones, especially today, when it is so easy to comparison shop with internet tools such as Yelp or online Consumer Reports available to consumers of virtually all products and services. A good brand name is a valuable asset to any business, perhaps its *most valuable* asset. Competition will not eliminate dishonesty, for there are sinners in all walks of life, but it does penalize dishonesty and rewards honesty in business dealings. Akerlof seemed oblivious to this ancient truth, as are all other "asymmetric information" theorists.

Friedrich Hayek, another Nobel laureate economist, spent much of his academic career researching and writing about the use of knowledge and information in society, so much so that a 2000 article in the *New Yorker* magazine called him "The Price Prophet" for having essentially anticipated the world of the internet (and its significance to society) decades before its actual appearance.[2] In a 1964 publication Hayek explained,

> We need to remember only how much we have to learn in any
> occupation after we have completed our theoretical training, how
> big a part of our working life we spend learning particular jobs,
> and how valuable an asset in all walks of life is knowledge of
> people, of local conditions, and of special circumstances.... The

A Book You're Not Supposed to Read

F. A. Hayek, *Individualism and Economic Order* (Chicago: University of Chicago Press, 1996).

The "Austrian School" Nobel laureate economist's most important essays, including "The Meaning of Competition," something many liberal economists seem to know so little about.

shipper who earns his living from using otherwise empty or half-filled journeys of tramp-steamers, or the [real] estate agent whose whole knowledge is almost exclusively one of temporary opportunities, or the *arbitrageur* who gains from local differences of commodity prices—are all performing eminently useful functions based on special knowledge of circumstances of the fleeting moment not known to others.[3]

In other words, it is the division of information in society—"asymmetric information," if you will—that makes the economic world go 'round. Consider this: Who knows more about home building—home builders or buyers? Who knows more about how to supply grocery stores with fresh meat—ranchers and farmers or consumers? Who knows more about manufacturing automobiles—automotive engineers or car purchasers? Who knows more about producing and selling clothing—clothing manufacturers and distributors or clothing shoppers?

The point of these questions is that *all* information about products and services in the marketplace is asymmetrical in successful capitalist countries because their success is based on the effective utilization of the division of labor *and knowledge* in society. If we all had symmetrical (that is, the same) information and knowledge, then none of these occupations—and very few of their products—would exist.

Economist Ludwig von Mises pinpointed the folly of the "asymmetric information" theory—some twenty years before Akerlof's article was published—in his renowned *Human Action: A Treatise on Economics*, first published in 1949.[4] Mises did not use the term "asymmetric information," but he discussed the same phenomenon. If everyone had the exact same knowledge about the economic world and acquired that information at the same time—the perfect world of nirvana posited by the asymmetric information theorists—it would be as though "every man is approached by an angel informing him of the change in [market] data."[5]

But even if "market participants" did have the same information about products, Mises wrote, they often appraise it differently. For example, you and I could have the exact same information about the quality of, say, a compact automobile. But if you value a compact car because of its good gas mileage and ease of parking and maneuvering in city traffic whereas I, at six foot four, have no use at all for a compact car, we will obviously value the car differently. In fact, different subjective evaluations of the exact same products and services are the main reason why *mutually advantageous* buying and selling takes place in an economy. Consider the used market for just about anything: say I think it's time to get rid of my old car and buy a new one, and my neighbor is looking for a relatively inexpensive used car for his teenage daughter. I'm willing to take my "bottom line price" of, say, $8,000, and my neighbor is willing to pay as much as, say, $10,000 for the car. If we strike a deal at $9,000, we are both happy with the deal, and both better off. I get a thousand bucks more than what the car was worth to me, and my neighbor pays a thousand less than what the car is worth to him. And his daughter gets a nice, clean used car.

A Book You're Not Supposed to Read

Ludwig von Mises, *The Anti-Capitalistic Mentality* (Auburn, Alabama: Mises Institute, 2016).

Mises theorizes about why so many in society hate the goose that lays their golden eggs while embracing prosperity-and soul-destroying socialism.

The Real Asymmetric Information Problem

Yes, buyers and sellers always have different amounts of information about products and services, but no, that differential is not a source of market failure. But there is another kind of asymmetric information problem that *does* cause failure. A subdiscipline of economics called "public choice" (discussed in detail in chapter 10 below) involves the use of economic theory and methods to study topics that were traditionally the domain of political scientists: elections, politicians, bureaucrats and bureaucracy, special-interest politics, and so forth.[6]

Several Nobel Prizes have been awarded to economists known for such research (such as James M. Buchanan, Gary Becker, and George Stigler). One of the elementary concepts of public choice is "rational ignorance." The idea is that the average person spends most of his or her time learning how to get through school, do a job, raise a family, buy a house, maintain a household, raise and educate children, pay the bills. Private affairs, in other words. Very few people, even TV news junkies, spend much time educating themselves on political affairs. We are rationally ignorant of most of what government does because, in the mind of the average citizen, the personal cost of becoming even a little more informed about government outweighs any conceivable benefit.

Indeed, it is impossible for the human mind to comprehend more than a tiny fraction of 1 percent of what government in America does these days. An A–Z list of U.S. government departments alone comprises over one thousand.[7] Most of them operate in secret, run by anonymous bureaucrats seemingly accountable to no one. If one adds state and local governments with all their departments, boards, special districts, "authorities," and so forth, there are thousands more. Just one function of the federal government—regulation—is catalogued every year by the Competitive Enterprise Institute, a Washington, D.C., think tank, in a publication called "Ten Thousand Commandments."[8] All new federal regulations are published in something called *The Federal Register.* As of 2021 there were 56,552 pages of tiny print listing all of the regulations, with about 24,000 new "public notices" of new regulations every year. How many of these have *you* researched? Any?

When your author taught the concept of rational ignorance to undergraduate economics students, he would ask who in the class could name his or her congressional representative and both U.S. senators. Even at a $50,000/year (and up) university, in a class of thirty or so students only two or three could typically answer the question. The students were not being bad or immoral or unpatriotic, only rational. And that was just naming a few politicians—I didn't ask about the details of any government policy.

A corollary to the rational-ignorance effect is that special-interest groups *do* make it their business to become very learned about policies that they benefit financially from and lobby for. Their superior knowledge—and their bribes in the form of "campaign contributions"—guarantee that government policies will be designed to put money in their pockets at the expense of the rationally ignorant taxpaying public. Democracy turns out to be one giant collection of policies whereby small in-the-know political minorities plunder the rationally ignorant majority day after day. That's the true "asymmetric information" at work in our economy and society.

This is especially true when it comes to foreign policy, which is always conducted in secret with relevant information zealously kept from the public in the name of "national security." Only "the intelligence community," comprising the CIA, FBI, NSA, and more than a dozen other intelligence-gathering government bureaucracies, is permitted to know what is going on. Whenever they are asked what they are up to, the typical answer is, "Sorry, that's classified information." Rational ignorance allows politicians to lie at will to the public, much more than all the dishonest car dealers in the world put together.

In competitive markets, dishonest businesspeople are eventually penalized with loss of business, bankruptcy, ruinous lawsuits, and even jail time for fraud. In government, at least at the federal level, one can have a fifty-year career of lying through one's teeth and suffer few, if any, negative consequences. This is because the electoral system is so rigged with gerrymandering and other monopolistic privileges—such as large staffs that are essentially taxpayer-funded permanent campaign staffs, and the ability to dole out millions in pork-barrel spending to one's congressional district or state—that congressional reelection rates have averaged over 90 percent for many decades.[9] If consumers are unhappy with what the market offers them, they can simply switch brands at any moment. Today they can do it online with lightning speed. In government, thanks to asymmetric information, *millions* of people can be grossly unhappy with what they are getting for their tax dollars and not be able to do a thing about it. Even if "throwing the bums out" at election time was a realistic option, members of Congress are in office for two years, senators for six, and presidents for four.

The real asymmetric information problem in society is with government, not markets, but somehow this has not caught the attention of the Ivy League gatekeepers of the economics profession, people like George Akerlof and Joseph Stiglitz (and their students), who always seem to be hard at work concocting the next theoretical nirvana fallacy.

CHAPTER 9

Creating Monopoly with Regulation

For more than a century, the standard approach to the economic study of government regulation has been the creation of various tales of market failure, followed by calls for government regulation "in the public interest" to supposedly correct the alleged failures of economic freedom. The basic idea has been that Adam Smith's famous "invisible hand" sometimes goes haywire because of self-interest and greed in the marketplace that create monopolies, "externalities," and so forth. Therefore, the theory goes, we need the intervention of benevolent, selfless "public servants" (that is, government regulatory bureaucrats) acting in the public interest, not their own private interests, to correct these problems.

It is a mystery how this theory was ever taken seriously, given the fact that students of politics have understood for literally thousands of years that government employees are no different from anyone else—they act in *their own* best interests, as they see them, just like everyone else—and their best interests are not always the same as the general public's interest. That is the very reason Thomas Jefferson famously stated that government needed to be bound by the "chains" of the Constitution, while James Madison, the "father of the Constitution," warned in *Federalist* no. 10 against what he called "the violence of faction," by which he meant normal, everyday special-interest politics in a democracy. The whole purpose of the Constitution, said Madison, was to limit and constrain such behavior. The founders certainly did not plan to hand over unlimited powers to the government, naively hoping that those powers would always be used "in the public interest." In another famous phrase, Madison pointed out that, after all, "If men were angels, no government would be necessary."[1]

The rulers you have today may be truly virtuous public servants, but there is no guarantee that that will *always* be true. Not every U.S. president is a George Washington. The theory of the selfless, benevolent, incorruptible "public servant" has always been a fairy tale—a fairy tale nonetheless enshrined in generations of textbooks (and not just economics textbooks). It is a finely tuned propaganda tool designed to get the public to acquiesce to more and more government control of their lives. It is also a repudiation of the political philosophy of the American founding fathers and their Constitution.

What else would one expect, after all, in an age of overwhelmingly government-funded and -dominated schooling administered by "progressives"? It is not at all unusual for school textbooks to portray government bureaucrats and politicians in this way, while rather harshly criticizing economic freedom, free enterprise, and civil society in general as plagued by "market failures," other inadequacies, and all forms of deplorable behavior.

Indeed, every time a crook or criminal in the business world is prosecuted for his crimes there is a chorus of academics who argue that such behavior is *inherent* in the system of economic freedom and call for more and more regulation of that system. There never seems to be any acknowledgment that there are sinners in all walks of life, not just the business world. Somehow the argument is never made that because a politician is discovered to be guilty of criminal behavior, therefore *all* politicians are

inherently criminal, or because *some* clergy-
men have committed crimes, then *all* clergy-
men are inherently suspect. It is typically only
businesspeople, as a class, who receive that
kind of treatment.

How Regulation Profits the Regulated and Harms Consumers

In reality, a great deal of government regulation of industry has been the result of lobbying
efforts *by the industry*. It is a well-known dic-
tum of economics that cartels—collections of
businesses that collude or conspire to act as one big monopoly by agreeing
to charge a single monopolistic price—invariably fall apart as a result of
"cheating." The incentive to cheat on any price-fixing agreement is overwhelming: if everyone else is charging one price, and a single business cuts
its price by, say, 50 percent, it will immediately make a killing, forcing all
the others to follow suit—or else. And they will. Even the notorious
Organization of the Petroleum Exporting Countries (OPEC) cartel, which
disrupted world oil markets in the 1970s, was effective for less than a
decade. This most famous of all cartels was created in 1960, but it wasn't
until 1973 that it was able to raise world oil prices.

Iran, Iraq, Kuwait, Saudi Arabia, Venezuela, Egypt, and Syria produced
a large percentage of the world's oil at that time. By severely reducing production they were able to quadruple the price of a barrel of oil from $3 to
$12 in a very short time. This was a classic example of cartel price-fixing.
It also became a classic example of the inherent instability of price-fixing
cartels—although it was a cartel of governments and not corporations.

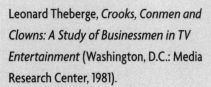

A Book You're Not Supposed to Read

Leonard Theberge, *Crooks, Conmen and Clowns: A Study of Businessmen in TV Entertainment* (Washington, D.C.: Media Research Center, 1981).

A "content analysis" of American TV that overwhelmingly portrayed businesspeople as, well, crooks, conmen, and clowns. Mur-
derers, as well.

Cheating on the price of oil prevailed from the very beginning, and by 1982 OPEC was effectively neutered as a result of the deregulation of oil prices in the United States, which caused an historic oil industry boom there. After all, the creation of monopoly profits in any industry will inevitably attract competitors, who will find a way to cash in on the situation. Oil from other countries, such as Great Britain, also caused oil prices to plunge, as OPEC's monopoly profits made it ever more profitable for others to invest in oil exploration.

There are many examples in history of industries *attempting* but *failing* to earn monopolistic profits by forming cartels because of cheating. There are just as many examples, however, of those same industries deciding that a more certain route to monopoly profits is through government regulation that *makes competition illegal.* The "natural monopoly" story told in chapter 8 is but one example. In the economics literature, thanks mostly to the Chicago School, there are myriad examples of what is known as the capture theory of regulation. In many instances, according to the theory, government regulatory agencies created ostensibly to regulate an industry "in the public interest" because of some kind of alleged "market failure" are routinely *captured* by the industries that they are supposed to be regulating for the benefit of the general public. From that point the agency issues regulations *for the benefit of the regulated industries* instead. After all, corporations and their well-funded lobbying operations are quite effective, whereas we consumers of their products are not politically organized at all.

There are many examples of regulatory capture, but it is also true that a great deal of government regulation was not actually captured but was in fact promoted by industry *in the first place* as a tool of monopolization. Rhetoric about the public interest has always been a political smokescreen. Even back in 1776, Adam Smith said in *The Wealth of Nations* that he had never known of much good done by a man who purported to trade in the public interest.

This has been true from the very beginning of the government regulation of industry in the United States. The first large federal regulatory agency was the Interstate Commerce Commission (ICC), created in 1887 supposedly to regulate the railroad industry. In the post–Civil War era there was a railroad-line building spree, as miles of track more than doubled in the single decade after the war.[2] Competition became fierce, and it caused passenger rates to plummet year after year. (The building of canals added even more competition in the transportation arena). Naturally, railroad corporations whined and complained bitterly about "cutthroat competition." They tried to create price-fixing cartels to prop up their prices and profits but failed miserably because of the powerful incentives to cheat on the agreements. Rebates were offered to favored customers in secret, for example, but were inevitably discovered by competitors, who would then cut their prices as well.[3]

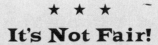

★ ★ ★

It's Not Fair!

The railroad corporations' complaint about too many competitors was like the New York Yankees' complaining bitterly that there are too many teams in Major League Baseball, unfairly depriving them of World Series wins.

All of this competition made some people unhappy, as it always does. When the railroad corporations offered quantity discounts or rebates to their largest customers (such as John D. Rockefeller's Standard Oil Company), the smaller customers who did not get the rebates complained. There was more competition—and more rail lines—for long-distance shipping than for shorter distances, so the short-distance shippers (including many farmers) complained that the short-haul rates were too high. All of these unsatisfied sour-grapes customers, led by politically organized farm organizations such as The Grange, started demanding government regulation of the railroads.

The railroad corporations cleverly became strong supporters of government regulation of their own businesses! They did this because they realized that 1) trying to form cartels was futile, and 2) they could use their

A Book You're Not Supposed to Read

Milton and Rose Friedman, *Free to Choose: A Personal Statement* (New York: Harcourt Brace Jovanovich, 1981).

The Friedmans' classic defense of free markets and critique of government intervention. It was also a PBS series.

political clout as the largest corporations in America to control any government regulatory agency for their own benefit and profits.

By the time the ICC was created, the political crusaders associated with the Granger movement had moved on to other issues, naively assuming that the ICC would operate to their benefit. They were immediately proven wrong, as the first commissioner of the ICC was one Thomas Cooley, a lawyer-lobbyist who had represented railroad corporations for many years.[4] Cooley immediately went to work lobbying Congress to give the ICC even greater regulatory powers over the railroad industry than the original law that created the ICC had. For example, it addressed the "problem" of long-haul rates being lower than short-haul rates by outlawing the lower rates! The railroad corporations rejoiced, while their customers were shafted. Over the years the ICC bureaucracy became staffed with "former" railroad employees who operated the agency essentially as a government cartel price-fixing enforcement agency.

In the 1920s an existential threat to the railroad industry's monopoly profits, which were protected by the ICC, emerged in the form of a vibrant long-distance trucking industry. The railroad corporations and the ICC immediately went to work to get the ICC to regulate trucking so that it could not compete too much with railroads. They succeeded with the Motor Carrier Act of 1933, which "gave the ICC jurisdiction over truckers—to protect the railroads, not the consumers," and "the railroad story was repeated for trucking. It was cartelized, its rates were fixed, routes assigned."[5]

Over the years trucking industry lobbyists came to dominate and replace the railroad industry lobbyists in control of the ICC. They got the ICC to require a "certificate of public convenience" in order to get a trucking license. As Milton and Rose Friedman wrote, as of 1980 "out of some 89,000 initial applications for such certificates after the passage of the Motor Carrier Act in 1935, the ICC approved only about 27,000."[6]

Some trucking companies were granted monopoly routes by the ICC, which also forced trucks to return from runs empty. For example, a trucker could ship a full load from, say, New York to Chicago, but was required by the ICC to return to the East Coast empty. In addition to being a waste of gas, the economic effect of this was to reduce the supply of trucking services, and the laws of supply and demand tell us that the result of that is higher trucking prices (and profits).

After more than a century of creating monopolies and enforcing price-fixing cartels in the railroad, trucking, bus line, and other industries, the ICC was abolished in 1995. It was such a blatant rip-off-the-consumer scam that there was bipartisan support in Congress for its demise.

Monopoly in the Sky

The history of government regulation of the airline industry is almost a carbon copy of the story of the regulation of railroads and trucking. In the beginning of the commercial airline industry, in the 1920s and early 1930s, there was fierce competition, the creation of nineteen airline companies, and of course the bankruptcy of some of them that were too inefficient and poorly managed to compete. As with railroads and trucking, many within the industry did not want to compete, and they had the example of how the ICC had been created by the railroad industry with the purpose of eliminating competition as much as possible. They chose the monopoly-through-government-regulation route to profits by supporting (and controlling) the Civil Aeronautics Board (CAB), founded in 1938.

The CAB copied the ICC recipe for monopoly by requiring government "certificates of public convenience" before any new airline could enter the business. With the incumbent airlines in political control of the CAB, there was little chance that many "certificates of public convenience" would ever be granted. Consequently, there were actually *fewer* airlines operating in the United States in 1978 than there had been in 1938![7]

The CAB dictated routes and rates, guaranteeing that the American airline industry would be operated as a centrally planned, lethargic, socialistic monopoly. The spirit of competition can never be fully eradicated, however (witness the black markets in the former Soviet Union), so when the CAB outlawed price-cutting, the airlines responded with other forms of non-price competition. They offered "free" food and alcoholic drinks, for example, after which the CAB even regulated the size of sandwiches that could be handed out on flights. Too much competition.

Because of the CAB-created airline cartel, air travel in the 1950s–1970s was prohibitively expensive for ordinary working-class Americans. The cost of all those sumptuous meals and "free" champagne served on flights was built into the ticket prices by the CAB regulators. Online images of "the golden age of air travel" show affluent men and women dressed in expensive-looking attire gorging themselves with steak, caviar, and lots and lots of alcohol.[8] There are also quite a few images of predominantly male passengers being served by young "stewardesses" dressed in miniskirts or "hot pants." Non-price competition in the airline business came in all forms and guises.

After four decades of stifling monopoly orchestrated by the airline industry's puppets at the CAB, some of the most notorious proponents of big government in America actually became the leading lights of the campaign to deregulate or abolish the CAB. Senator Ted Kennedy, who spent his entire career assuring that the government in Washington would be as bloated as possible, was a leader of the movement to abolish the CAB during the Carter administration. Even Ralph Nader supported it, so blatant was the CAB cartel-enforcing scam. The Civil Aeronautics Board was finally abolished by the United States Airline Deregulation Act of 1978. By 1990, average fares had declined by 30 percent in real inflation-adjusted dollars, saving travelers billions of dollars.[9] All of a sudden, discounted tickets—discounted by as much as 65 percent from the posted fares—appeared.

Newly unleashed competition caused large improvements in airline productivity and allowed airlines to serve markets that they were not previously permitted to serve by their CAB overseers. Air travel also became "unequivocally safer than it was before deregulation," thanks to competition.[10] Not to mention that car travel is more dangerous, statistically speaking, than air travel. Getting people out of long-distance car travel and into airplanes instead literally saved lives.

The airlines are still heavily regulated by the Federal Aviation Administration and the U.S. Department of Transportation, and most major airports are operated by municipal government bureaucracies. This government involvement in the airline industry remains the main cause of inefficiencies, slowdowns, and other problems in air travel, which are typical of all heavily regulated industries. The airline corporations themselves are largely responsible for this: in accepting government bailouts after the Great Recession of 2008, for example, they agreed to ever more regulatory requirements, proving once again the ancient adage that "he who takes the king's shilling becomes the king's man." Nevertheless, the nature of regulation is no longer to create a cartel price-fixing scheme with iron-handed governmental coercion, as it was under CAB regulation.

Many other federal regulatory agencies have been captured by the industries they are supposed to be regulating "in the public interest." Milton and Rose Friedman wrote that the story of the ICC (and CAB) "illustrates what might be called the *natural* history of government intervention" [emphasis added] through regulation:[11]

> A real or fancied evil leads to demands to do something about it.
> A political coalition forms consisting of sincere, high-minded

reformers and equally sincere interested parties. The incompatible objectives of the members of the coalition (e.g., low prices to consumers and high prices to producers) are glossed over by fine rhetoric about "the public interest," "fair competition," and the like. The coalition succeeds in getting Congress (or a state legislature) to pass a law. The preamble to the law pays lip service to the rhetoric and the body of the law grants power to government officials to "do something." The high-minded reformers experience a glow of triumph and turn their attention to new causes. The interested parties [i.e., airline corporations, railroad corporations] go to work to make sure that the power is used for *their* benefit. They generally succeed. [Emphasis added.][12]

Perhaps the most captured of all government agencies is the Food and Drug Administration (FDA), whose mission seems to be exclusively to increase the profits of the pharmaceutical industry. Clear evidence of this is a report of who was on an FDA advisory panel that voted to permit COVID vaccines for children between the ages of 5 and 11 in 2021 despite the fact that the probability of a child dying from COVID was essentially zero (and there were reports of serious negative side effects of the vaccine itself). A report at the website Zero Hedge described the FDA advisory committee in this way:

[T]he meeting roster shows that numerous members of the committee and temporary voting members have worked for [pharmaceutical corporation] Pfizer or have major connections to Pfizer. Members include a former vice president of Pfizer vaccines, a recent Pfizer consultant, a recent Pfizer research grant recipient, a man who mentored a current top Pfizer vaccine executive, a man who runs a center that gives out Pfizer vaccines, the chair of a Pfizer data group, a guy who was proudly photographed taking a Pfizer vaccine, and numerous people who are already on the record supporting coronavirus vaccines for children. Meanwhile, recent FDA commissioner Scott Gottlieb is on Pfizer's board of directors.[13]

★ ★ ★
Cat Gets the Cream

A non-political head of a government agency is as realistic as a meowing dog.

Is it any wonder that the vaccines were approved? On top of this kind of revolving door between government and industry is the fact that in the 1980s a federal law was passed that gave the pharmaceutical corporations legal immunity from lawsuits related to their vaccines.[14] They cannot be sued for negative side effects, including death, from their vaccines. What other industry has been granted legal immunity from lawsuits related to its products even if they literally kill its customers?

It should be added that every time there is a crisis caused by government intervention—such as the Great Recession of 2008, caused by a housing market bubble orchestrated by the Federal Reserve Board and other government agencies, including Congress—"reformers" will uniformly clamor for *more* government regulation and other forms of intervention.[15] The inevitable result will be *more* government-protected monopolies, more political cronyism, and more government-induced economic crises. The world has yet to discover the angelic, selfless, benevolent, non-political head of a federal regulatory agency. One does not get appointed to such a position by being non-political.

Closer-to-Home Regulated Monopolies

Regulation—primarily state and local government regulation—has also been used to create monopoly power in literally thousands of other industries. A key example is occupational licensing regulation. While a case can be made that many such regulations have a safety component to them, such as requiring doctors to have a medical degree from an accredited medical school, it is undeniable that others have had the intent and the effect of blocking competition into the field for the benefit of the incumbent practitioners and at the expense of their customers and potential competitors.

The classic example of this phenomenon is New York City's regulation of taxicab services, which began in 1937. At that time the city government sold licenses called "medallions" to all existing 13,566 cab drivers.[16] Very few additional medallions were ever issued. The effect of this system was to essentially outlaw any new legal competition for existing cab companies and drivers. As the population of New York City increased (along with the number of tourists and business travelers), the demand for taxicab services skyrocketed over the years, while the number of legal taxicabs remained constant. Exploding demand for cab services combined with no increase at all in the supply of cab services caused the price of cab fare—and the cost of a medallion—to increase as well.

The owners of the cab companies that had existed in 1937 were the main beneficiaries of this system, as they only paid a measly $10 for their medallions. By 2013 the price of a New York City taxi medallion had risen from its original $10 to $1.3 million.[17] Dozens of other cities also have their own versions of New York City taxi licensing, but none was ever as extreme. Of course, the more any business is isolated from competition, the lower the quality of the product or service that it provides. Occupational licensing regulation of this type gives consumers less for more money, in other words. As of this writing there are over five hundred occupations licensed by state and local governments.[18]

Even regulation can never create a *permanent* monopoly, however; technology often foils the best-laid schemes of monopolists and their political sponsors. In the case of taxicab monopolies, the advent of ride-sharing companies such as Uber and Lyft ended the taxi cartels in New York City and virtually everywhere else, causing catastrophic losses to all those New York medallion owners. Illegal, unlicensed, or "gypsy" cabs had existed for quite a while, but it was the entrance of Uber and Lyft onto the market that finally ended the regulation-protected taxi monopolies.

As with railroad, trucking, airline, and all other kinds of regulation, various "public interest" rationales are routinely given for occupational licensing regulation—including arguments about protecting the public from monopoly (!), or dangerous products, or unsavory characters (just how savory are the enforcers of monopolistic occupational licensing regulation, though?). And as with the other types of regulation, incumbents who are already in the business typically use the regulation as a barrier to new competitors.

Regulators Turned Lobbyists Turned Millionaires

The phrase "revolving door" in politics refers to the way bureaucrats, members of Congress, and their staffs are responsible for regulating various industries in their "public service" jobs and then leave those jobs to work in the industries—and "earn" millions. They spend their time in government enforcing the cartel pricing regulations and other forms of hidden subsidies to businesses, and then they cash in as contractors or employees of the corporations they used to regulate or as lobbyists lobbying the government agents who used to be their colleagues.[19] The revolving door guarantees that the monopoly-creating, regulatory racket will go on indefinitely.

A 2006 *Washingtonian* magazine article entitled "Washington in the Money: How Washington Got Really Rich" celebrated the wealth created in the nation's capital by the revolving door.[20] The article highlighted former congressman Billy Tauzin of Louisiana as a typical example. Tauzin "cashed out" by leaving Congress for a pharmaceutical industry job as a lobbyist paying $2.3 million a year.

"Big money wealth has become so commonplace that it is no longer special" in Washington, D.C., the magazine crowed. At that time, the city boasted more than 55,000 homes worth more than $1 million owned by "everyday millionaires" whose net worth was between $2 million and $10 million; "[r]ich but don't know it types," who were worth between $10 million and $50 million; and 7,200 "really rich" who made more than $500 million annually. And then there were 500 or so "tycoon rich" whose net worth was at least $1 billion. The magazine described some Washington, D.C., neighborhoods as having "streets of gold," where houses were going for $3 million and up. Apparently there's a lot of money to be made in selflessly promoting "the public interest."

CHAPTER 10

The Economics of Government Failure

For most of the twentieth century, the economics profession was obsessed with the nirvana fallacy and invented innumerous theories of "market failure." The analysis was always accompanied by recommendations for taxation, regulation, government subsidies, government mandates, price controls, or other forms of government interventionism and central planning to fix supposed market failure problems. It was simply assumed that government bureaucrats, instructed and funded by the not-so-invisible-hands of politicians, would be, well, perfect. Perfect politicians and bureaucrats would fix the problems created by imperfect markets—in other words, the behavior of people like yourself and your author.

Beginning in the late 1950s and 1960s a group of economists, many associated with the University of Chicago, began to revive the limited-constitutional-government thinking of the American founders as it applied to economic analysis. They invented a whole new subdiscipline called "public choice" which was essentially the application of economic theory and methodology to the study of *political* decision-making.[1] The topics they researched and wrote about were traditional political science topics—elections, lobbying, special-interest groups, bureaucracy, and so forth—but the methodology was from the field of economics.

A man who leaves the business world and is elected to public office does not sprout an angel's halo and become a virtual Mother Teresa; nor does he grow devil's horns and necessarily become corrupt or incompetent. Like everyone else, politicians want to keep their jobs, get promoted to higher offices, and generally prosper. This motivation guides their behavior, says public choice analysis. The result is that while government may do many things that benefit the general public (maintaining law and order, defending against foreign invaders, enforcing the rule of law, and the like), there are also many reasons that *government failure* is inherent, and it can be far more harmful to society than any market failure. If, say, the market for used cars is "imperfect," that's one thing, but it only affects used-car buyers. When the central government imposes a failed policy on the entire nation, then the failure affects the entire nation and not just one small market.

The two economists who are most responsible for founding the field of public choice, or the economics of government failure, are your author's graduate school professors (and onetime George Mason University colleagues) James M. Buchanan and Gordon Tullock.[2] Buchanan was awarded the Nobel Prize in Economics in 1986 for his role in founding the public choice school within the economics profession.[3] Nobel laureates George Stigler and Gary Becker were also cited by the Nobel committee for research they had done in the area of the economics of politics or public choice.

Government's Inherent Failures

James Buchanan coined the phrase "political externalities" to describe the inevitable harm imposed upon political minorities as a part of the normal democratic process. He made the obvious point that government policies (whether to "correct" market failures or for any other purpose) are not made by benevolent and omniscient dictators but by voters, special-interest groups, legislators, and all other actors in the political process. Think of the usual left-right continuum that is talked about in politics, with the far left comprising communists who want totalitarian government, and the extreme right being anarchists who want no government at all. Most people are somewhere around the middle of this continuum. That means that in order to win elections political candidates must cater to the wishes of the middle-of-the-road or median voter (the "median voter" has as many other voters to his left as to his right ideologically).

This means that everyone to the right of the middle-of-the-road voter who wants less government, lower taxes, less regulation, and so forth is unhappy. It also means that people to the left of the median voter are unhappy because they want higher taxes (usually for others, not themselves) and bigger government. This unhappiness, which is a normal and inevitable result of majority-rule elections in a democracy, is what Buchanan called "political externalities."

Elections are all-or-none decisions. Once one candidate is voted into office or one policy is voted into place, it applies to *everyone*. You can wear a T-shirt that say "Mr. X Is Not My President" as a protest, but Mr. X (or Mrs. X) is indeed your president, whether or not you voted for him (or her).

This state of affairs is in sharp contrast to the marketplace, where everyone gets what he or she wants by "voting" with dollars. If I want a hamburger, and you want a salad, then fine, we each get what we want. If we use democracy to determine what's for dinner and hamburger wins, then everyone has to have hamburger for dinner and all the vegetarians are very unhappy (and hungry). Thus voluntary free-market exchange is unanimous, in the sense that buyer and seller agree in every transaction—or else no transaction takes place. Government in a democracy is *never* unanimous and is therefore always plagued with political externalities. The vast majority of all government policies create winners and losers. And because the perceived benefits of government policies are so subjective—a matter of *opinion*—there is no way even to determine whether the benefits to the "winners" outweigh the costs to the "losers." But losers they are, thanks to the tyranny of the majority, as James Madison explained in *Federalist* no. 51.[4]

This was the thinking behind the creation of the uniquely American system of federalism: at the beginning of the republic, most governmental powers were at the state and local levels, and government was highly decentralized. (It is also the idea behind the highly decentralized Swiss governmental system.) If an American suffers from too many political externalities in one town, city, or state, he can "vote with his feet" and move to another jurisdiction, where there are more like-minded voters. You don't have to live in big-government New York or California; you can move to smaller-government Florida or Texas.

Beginning around the time of the American Civil War, the history of government became a history of consolidation and centralization of power—in Washington, D.C., London, Paris, Berne, and all national capitals. Socialism in the Soviet Union and China and fascism in Italy and Germany were the high-water mark of highly centralized, bureaucratic government. The more centralized governments become, the more political externalities there are, and the less capable the people will be of influencing their government. It has long been recognized that the average citizen has more of a chance of influencing his local town government than his state government, and certainly his national government. And centralized power causes government failure on steroids, for this and other reasons we will discuss. The "political externalities" resulting from the tyranny of the majority comprise just one category of government failure in the literature of public choice.

Why Special Interests Rule

In reality, even the majority is rarely satisfied with the results of government since so much of what governments do is the result of special-interest politics. Minority rule, or the tyranny of the minority, is even more pervasive than tyranny of the majority. One reason is so-called logrolling, or vote trading. Take, for example, a small community with, say, thirty thousand residents who are divided on the issues of raising taxes to help finance schools and hospitals. Let's assume that ten thousand are younger residents who favor spending more on schools but not any more on the local hospital. Another group of ten thousand consist of older people who favor more spending on hospitals but, since their children are grown, do not want to spend any more on schools. A third group wants to spend nothing more on either schools or hospitals. So the breakdown is like this:

Group A	Group B	Group C
Schools but Not Hospital	Hospital but Not Schools	Neither One

If the local voting rule requires a two-thirds majority to raise taxes for more spending on schools or hospitals, a referendum on school spending will fail because Group A will be for it, but B and C oppose it. If there is a referendum on raising taxes to spend more on the hospital Group B will be for it but A and C oppose it. The true preference of the community, then, from a democratic majority-rule perspective, is to maintain the status quo and spend no more on anything.

How "logrolling" works is that representatives of, say, Group A will approach Group B's representatives and say, *Look, we don't want to pay more taxes for the hospital, but we will bite the bullet and vote for your referendum if, in return, you vote for our referendum to raise taxes for schools when it comes up—even though you don't want to spend any more of your tax dollars on schools.* A deal is struck, resulting in more spending on both schools and hospitals, even though the true preference of the majority is no more taxing and spending on anything.

Logrolling is what members of legislatures do all day long while the legislature is in session. It is routine to see a representative from the inner city voting for a farm subsidy bill despite there not being a single farmer in his or her district. The vote is likely the result of a vote trade whereby he promised to vote for the farm bill in exchange for rural representatives' voting for urban renewal spending, despite there not being any urban areas in their districts. With logrolling, what politics gives us is not rule by a majority but special-interest legislation, each piece of which benefits a small minority at the expense of the taxpaying majority.

And there is yet another reason that numerical minorities rule in "majority rule" democracies: most legislation benefits relatively small, concentrated, and politically active groups, while the tax bill for the benefits is widely dispersed among the general taxpaying population. Take, for example, farm subsidies. A few dozen agricultural corporations may receive millions from the U.S. Treasury, but each taxpayer will contribute only a few dollars (or pennies). The benefits are concentrated in the small number of farm businesses, and the average taxpayer has no idea that his or her taxes are a little higher because of it. Thus the taxpayers have no incentive to oppose the program, despite the fact that it is nothing but corporate welfare for already well-to-do agricultural corporations.

This is just one example, but there are thousands and thousands of government programs of all kinds that do just this: distribute concentrated benefits to politically potent special-interest groups at the expense of the general public. When the steel industry, for example, lobbies for tariffs on imported steel, the result is that American-made steel becomes more expensive. If every ton of steel that is imported from another country has a special tax attached to it, that allows American steel manufacturers to raise their prices and increase their profits. Everything made of steel becomes more expensive, but the cost of this indirect subsidy to the steel industry (stockholders, managers, owners, employees) is widely dispersed in the American population. The average car may be only a few hundred dollars more expensive, for example. And the average "rationally ignorant" person is clueless about why his new car costs more than the same model did just last year.

A Book You're Not Supposed to Read

Gordon Tullock, Gordon Brady, and Arthur Seldon, *Government Failure: A Primer in Public Choice* (Washington, D.C. Cato Institute, 2002).

Public choice economics explained by one of its inventors and one of his former students.

"Rational ignorance" does not apply to the beneficiaries of special-interest politics, however. The recipients of farm subsidies or tariffs on steel will become very well informed indeed on the subject—and use their expertise to lobby the government to maintain and expand the subsidies. In addition, they will typically produce a fog of propaganda to convince the public that taxing lower- and middle-income Americans so that wealthy corporate agribusinesses can be showered with subsidies is somehow in the interest of lower- and middle-income taxpayers. Or that forcing lower- and middle-income citizens to pay more for their next new car (thanks to tariffs on imported cars) is somehow in *their* best interest. Buy American! Save the family farm! Support American manufacturing! So not only are people rationally ignorant of the vast majority of the government's often mind-bogglingly arcane legislation; much of what people think they know about it is self-serving propaganda (in other words, lies) produced by the beneficiaries of special-interest legislation.

The Short-Sightedness of Politics

Critics of private enterprise are constantly complaining about the alleged short-sightedness of corporate executives, with their concentration on the last quarter's profits. The implication is that the nature of business is that the future is ignored in the focus on the short-term bottom line.

First of all, it is a *good* thing that business managers are focused on their bottom line because voluntary trade is mutually beneficial to buyers and sellers, and the more business is successful, the more prosperity there will be all around. And the more prosperity, the more job security there will be. Moreover, the same leftists who charge private enterprise with being too short-sighted also complain that there are too many big corporations that have been "at the top" (in terms of profitability) far too long. But one does not become a long-term highly profitable company by being short-sighted and ignoring the future. Quite the contrary, especially in today's information economy, where it is imperative to keep innovating to cut costs, improve service, and create new valued products—or else. Those companies that fail to invest in enough research and development to maintain their competitiveness will go bankrupt or be acquired by someone else who *will* do those things.

The real short-sightedness problem in society is in government. At the federal level every member of Congress must run for reelection every two years and every senator every six years. Their focus is always on the next election, which, for the U.S. House of Representatives, is always just around the corner. This produces an incentive to vote for government subsidies and other benefits that will be dispensed to constituents right now, today, in time for the upcoming election. That is why there is always quite a government spending binge in the three-to-six-month period leading up to every election.

Voting to spend taxpayers' dollars on their constituents makes incumbent politicians more popular and wins them votes, but raising taxes to pay for it all will lose them votes. That's why politicians of all parties are deficit-spending hogs, voting to spend money now to assure their reelection, and paying for it by incurring even more government debt through borrowing, so that the cost of government programs becomes essentially invisible. Not free, for nothing is free, but disguised. It's called "fiscal illusion." When the government borrows by selling bonds, the cost of today's spending is delayed and dispersed, as future taxpayers are on the hook for the principal and interest on the bonds.

Borrowing makes sense for infrastructure programs like roads or sewer lines that provide benefits for twenty to thirty years or longer, but hundreds of billions or trillions of dollars in federal spending that is financed through borrowing goes to transfer payments—money given to individuals and institutions today that is not for long-term infrastructure of any kind. Government borrowing to finance current transfer payments is a trick designed to fool the public into believing that government is like Santa Claus and can give it something for nothing.

★ ★ ★
Peace Dividend

Thomas Jefferson espoused the idea that government's borrowing for infrastructure, or to finance a defensive war, was necessary and proper, but it should be limited to a single generation, which he believed was about twenty years. It would be immoral, he believed, for one generation to impose a tax burden on a future generation, which would be, by definition, politically defenseless against such plunder. He also believed that "half the world's wars" would be avoided if each generation had to pay off the government debt that it incurred for the wars.[5]

Legalized Plunder

The "market failure" theorists have always been obsessed with "efficiency" and "social welfare," which they claim are harmed when markets fall short of utopian fantasies (the nirvana fallacy). It is the political process itself, however, that causes gigantic inefficiencies in society. Particularly in today's world, when so much of what governments do involves transfer payments from one group of citizens to another. The transfer payments do not arise randomly out of thin air, any more than the laws and regulations

★ ★ ★

The Mot Juste

Your author prefers "plunder-seeking" to "rent-seeking" because it is more descriptive. All of the above examples involve one group of citizens using the coercive powers of the state to (legally) plunder fellow citizens.

that create monopoly profits. They are all lobbied for by the potential beneficiaries.

There are, after all, only three ways to make money: 1) producing and selling goods and services to your fellow man (and woman), 2) lobbying governments for transfer payments from others, or for some kind of monopolistic privilege, and 3) theft. Regarding the first two options, think of it this way. If one is in, say, the mousetrap business, one way of making money is to produce better mousetraps than the competition. Another way of making money would be to lobby the legislature to ban the importation of all foreign-made mousetraps. The latter would reduce the supply of mousetraps, driving up prices and profit levels.

In the first instance, consumers get something in return for their money—a better mousetrap. In the second instance consumers get less than nothing: they pay more for the same old mousetrap. In fact, with weakened competitive pressures, the quality of the mousetrap will probably decline, leaving the consumer paying more for less.

The same analysis would apply in the case of corporations and unions lobbying for any kind of government protection, government subsidy, or government-created monopoly status: a cable TV company lobbying for a monopoly franchise in a city; public school teachers' unions lobbying to prevent competition from charter schools or school vouchers; windmill manufacturers lobbying for government subsidies for their windmill businesses; and on and on.

This political process—the process of influencing government to cause an income transfer or the creation of monopoly profits (with no benefits for consumers)—has been given the clunky name of "rent-seeking" by the economics profession. "Rent" has a different meaning to economists than it does to normal people. It is not what is paid to a landlord. Economic "rent" is payment for some resource that is more than what would be paid for it in a competitive free market. For example, if mousetraps go for $1 each and then all foreign mousetraps are banned by protectionist legislation, the supply of mousetraps will decline and their price will rise to, say, $2. The extra dollar caused by the protectionist legislation is the economic rent.

The process of lobbying government, and all the time and money spent on it, is what is called "rent-seeking." It is a gargantuan diversion of society's human and physical resources away from working and producing goods and services that are of value to one's fellow citizens to plundering those same fellow citizens though some kind of governmental scam. Money for nothing, in other words.

Another important phrase in economics is "opportunity cost": the value of the best alternative to the course of action that one decides to take. If I spend $1000 on a vacation, the opportunity cost is what else I could have spent that money on. If a lawyer bills clients at $100 per hour, every workday hour that he takes off to play golf has a $100 opportunity cost. The opportunity cost of rent-seeking is that all of that time, money, and energy could alternatively have been spent actually producing more, better, or cheaper products for consumers and making money that way. Over the long run, a "rent-seeking society" will encourage fewer people to become educated in engineering and other productive professions, and more people to become lawyers, lobbyists, and publicists instead—the instruments of rent-seeking instead of the instruments of production, in other words. Some may benefit and even become enormously wealthy through rent-seeking, but the rest of society is poorer and more backward as a result of it.

Economist Mancur Olson was known for arguing that rent-seeking was a major deterrent to economic development in poorer countries and that the decline or abolition of rent-seeking was a key to greater prosperity in such

A Book You're Not Supposed to Read

Mancur Olson, *The Rise and Decline of Nations* (New Haven, Connecticut: Yale University Press, 1984).

How the abolition of government intervention and special-interest politics have historically caused prosperity and the "rise of nations."

★ ★ ★

Rent-Seeking Pushed to Its Logical Conclusion

In the extreme case, as F. A. Hayek once said, in a socialist society the only power worth having is political power.

societies. He even ascribed the rapid success of the Japanese economy after World War II to the fact that the old prewar political regime of massive cronyism and rent-seeking had been wiped out and replaced with free markets and a much greater degree of economic freedom, allowing a work ethic to supplant a rent-seeking ethic.[6]

Economists James Gwartney, Randall Holcombe, and Robert Lawson published an important study on how the growth of government—and also the composition of government (that is, *how* it spends taxpayers' dollars)—affects economic growth and prosperity.[7] They noted that all during the twentieth century the "core functions" of government, such as police; the judiciary; the criminal justice system; national defense; education; highways; and sewage treatment, sanitation, and environmental protection, became smaller and smaller percentages of total government expenditures in dozens of countries around the world, including the United States. Government transfer payments of all kinds, on the other hand, skyrocketed, especially in the second half of the century. They documented that the growth of government in this way—which enabled a more or less exponential growth in rent-seeking activities—caused lower economic growth and less prosperity across the board. It also caused a redistribution of income from the general public to the politically connected.

Paying More for Less: Government Bureaucracy

Whenever government bureaucracies take over a function that can be provided by private, competitive businesses, the inevitable result is a decline in quality and an increase—sometimes an extreme increase—in cost. The words "bureaucrat" and "bureaucracy" have negative connotations for a good reason. No one likes to be called a "bureaucrat" or his methods "bureaucratic."

Government bureaucracies are so notoriously inefficient not because the people who work in government bureaucracies are lazy, incompetent, or corrupt. There are lazy, incompetent, and corrupt people in the private business world—and everywhere else. The reason for bureaucratic inefficiency is the incentive system in government, which is vastly different from the incentive system in private, competitive markets. In the private sector there is a market-feedback mechanism: businesses that please their customers with good (and improved) products at competitive prices are rewarded with profits; businesses that fail to do so are punished with losses or bankruptcy. This doesn't guarantee good products and services at reasonable prices, but it certainly establishes an incentive system to maximize the likelihood of that result.

Profits and losses are the measuring rods of how good a job a business is doing with regard to serving its customers. Growing profits mean that a better and better job is being done in that regard; losses mean the opposite. No one is forced to buy anything from anyone in a free market. Every person on the planet is perfectly free to say to the wealthiest business in the world, *No thanks, I think your product stinks.* (In sharp contrast, you may think that *government* "services" stink to high heaven, but you still have to pay for them with taxes—or you will be sent to prison for tax evasion.)

There are no profit-and-loss statements in government, so there is no way of telling whether or not governmental "customers" are being served well

A Book You're Not Supposed to Read

Ludwig von Mises, *Bureaucracy* (Indianapolis: Liberty Fund, 2007).

Mises explains the difference between profit management (capitalism) and bureaucratic management (by government)—if the latter can even be called "management" and not mismanagement.

or poorly. There are only budgets. And those budgets come with incentives that are exactly the opposite of the incentives in the private sector. Government bureaucrats are not rewarded for cutting costs (and taxes) or improving the quality of service, nor are they penalized for letting costs get out of control and providing poor-quality services. If there is money left over in the annual budget because of any cost-cutting, it is illegal to share it with government bureaucrats in the form of bonuses or profit-sharing, as in the private sector. The end-of-the-year budget incentive is perverse in that, if there ever should be money left over, it will be more difficult for an agency to make a case for a bigger budget the next year, since each agency competes with other government agencies for funding. So there is an end-of-the-budget-year spending binge in every government bureaucracy to make sure that every last penny is spent (or wasted).[8]

Because of civil service laws and regulations, it is extremely difficult to fire an incompetent government bureaucrat. Faced with the prospect of spending a significant part of one's budget on lawyers and years in court over the firing of one employee, government managers often get rid of embarrassingly incompetent employees with their only alternative course of action—offering them a pay raise and promotion to another government job in another part of the bureaucracy. Public school administrative offices in some cities are packed with teachers who were failures in the classroom and were eventually shunted off to the central administrative office (with a hefty pay increase), where they participate in the administration of the entire school system.

Government bureaucracies either are monopolies by legislation or are given unfair advantages over their private-sector competitors. Private schools may compete with public schools in any city, for example, but the public schools have all of their capital and payroll costs paid for by taxpayers. This is one reason why the concept of "businesslike" government is nonsensical. Politicians are fond of promising to operate government bureaucracies more like private businesses, but what business has all of its expenses paid for by taxpayers under threat of imprisonment?! What business could survive for half a century or longer, as Amtrak has, without ever making a profit in any single year?

Business and government simply do not work the same way: the incentives are diametrically opposed. Since promotions, pay, and other rewards are not based on profitability in the government sector, the number of subordinates that one manages becomes the measuring rod of achievement. This obviously creates incentives for government agency managers to increase the number of employees who work under them. It is not unusual for governments to use several times the labor to perform the same tasks that private businesses perform.

In government bureaucracies, failure is success. The worse the public schools get, the more money they get in next year's budget. The longer government fails in its War on Poverty, the more money the poverty agencies get. The longer the failed wars that are never won go on, the more enriched is the Pentagon and the military-industrial establishment. And on and on. This is because government and its supporters in the media and elsewhere have the power to drown out most other voices about its failures, and to keep repeating that its failures are in reality the fault of the stingy taxpayers who refuse to give it enough money to do the job right, even as the job is done poorly decade after decade, through repeated boosts in spending. This is how and why failure in government is *rewarded* financially—exactly the opposite of the market-feedback mechanism in the private business world. The worst thing that could happen to the government poverty bureaucracy would be the end of poverty.

A Book You're Not Supposed to Read

William Niskanen, *Bureaucracy and Representative Government* (London: Routledge, 2007).

The classic explanation of why government bureaucrats tend to be cost maximizers—unlike profit-seeking businesses, which strive to *minimize* costs.

Many studies have been published over the years comparing government agencies to private enterprises that produce the same service. One survey concluded that whenever government performs a function that could be performed by private competitive enterprises instead, the cost will double, on average, and quality of service will decline.[9] A comprehensive survey of privatization of government services in over one hundred countries concurred that the typical result was significant cost reduction and quality improvement.[10]

Every government bureaucrat is a budget maximizer (which is to say, a cost-of-government-service maximizer), regardless of his or her motivation. If the motivation is cynical and selfish—having a bigger budget to hire more subordinates in order to set yourself up for a bigger position in the government, or simply to have more to spend on assistants or lavish office furnishings—it takes a bigger budget. If the motivation is completely benevolent and charitable—to save the world from some kind of problem or danger, for example—then a bigger budget is also required. The successful government bureaucrat will become an expert at political manipulation, propaganda, and self-promotion (as opposed to being an expert at producing a product or service) to that end.

One implication is that government bureaucracies tend to be filled with crisis-mongers, people who are constantly warning of a crisis, real or imagined, if—you guessed it—their budget is not increased. (Their work is made easier by the fact that the public is, as we have seen, "rationally ignorant" of most of what government does, and bureaucrats do an expert job of posing as indispensable experts.) This kind of thinking was perfectly illustrated by a now-famous statement by Rahm Emanuel, President Barack Obama's chief of staff, in 2008, when he said publicly, "You never let a good crisis go to waste." The Great Recession of 2008, he was suggesting, was a golden opportunity for advocates of unlimited Big Government like himself and his boss, the president, to achieve what they could not ordinarily achieve in more normal economic times.

Economic historian Robert Higgs's book *Crisis and Leviathan: Critical Episodes in the Growth of American Government* provides chapter and verse of how government bureaucrats have played various crises like finely tuned fiddles in their quest for ever-more bloated budgets.[11] The book discusses late nineteenth-century economic crises, the Progressive Era of the early twentieth century, both World Wars, and the Great Depression. It is an exposition of what has long been known as the "ratchet effect" of government growth in crises. Once there is a crisis—real or perceived—governments stir up hysteria over the crisis, disarming political opposition to their plans for higher taxes, more debt, more regulations, more mandates and controls, and more spending. The frightened public not only acquiesces but demands that government "do something" to alleviate the crisis (which, as for example in the case of the Great Depression, the government itself may have created). As Randolph Bourne wrote in his famous World War I essay "War Is the Health of the State," in a crisis like a war, most people "allow themselves to be regimented, coerced, deranged in all the environments of their lives."[12] This phenomenon does not just apply to the crisis of war; the "pandemic" of 2020–2021 would seem to be the perfect fit as well.

The size and scope of government ratchets up. Then the war is over, or the depression is ended, but the size and scope of government never goes all the way back down to its pre-crisis level.

A Book You're Not Supposed to Read

Robert Higgs, *Crisis and Leviathan: Critical Episodes in the Growth of American Government* (New York: Oxford University Press, 1987).

Governmental powers always ratchet up (and freedom declines) during real or imaginary crises, but they never ratchet fully back down when the crisis is over.

Government bureaucrats are consummate political game players. One of their favorite games is what is known as the "Washington Monument Syndrome."[13] The phrase comes from an episode in the 1960s when the director of the federal government's National Park Service did not get as large a budget from Congress as he desired, and he responded by shutting down the Washington Monument, the most popular tourist attraction in Washington, D.C. Members of Congress were deluged with angry phone calls from constituents from all states who had traveled to Washington, D.C., for a family vacation and wanted to voice their anger and disappointment that the Washington Monument had been temporarily closed. The Park Service got its budget request.

After that experience, it seems that the same game has been played by all government bureaucrats everywhere, at all levels of government. Deny the police their budget request, and the cops walk out and ambulance services are shut down. Deny the public school teachers' union their pie-in-the-sky wage increase request, and they go on strike, or the school system suddenly runs out of money for school buses. Disagree with the Public Works Department's demands, and no garbage gets collected. Until, of course, the elected officials "come to their senses" and cave in to bureaucratic extortion. Never is it admitted that such shutdowns can be avoided by cutting costs somewhere else—something that private enterprises are forced to do every day.

CHAPTER 11

Who Creates Jobs?
(And Who Destroys Them?)

In the early 1980s your author was invited to speak to a room full of journalists in Washington, D.C., at an event sponsored by conservative journalistic icon M. Stanton Evans and the National Journalism Center. The topic was how to create jobs, since the U.S. economy had just suffered through years of "stagflation"—the simultaneous increase in inflation and unemployment. It was a bit shocking for an economist to hear that the Washington, D.C., journalists in the room were completely clueless as to how jobs—even their own jobs—were created. They kept asking, "Who creates jobs?" The response by yours truly was for them to look at who signed their own paychecks, for starters—that would inform them about who had created *their* jobs.

In general, it is entrepreneurs, capitalists, employers, investors, and business managers—the "capitalist class"—that are the sole source of job creation in any economy. Governments do not create any jobs at all because they must first destroy jobs and potential jobs by commandeering resources from the private sector with taxation, borrowing, mandates, and the creation of money out of thin air via the Federal Reserve Board, which controls the nation's money supply. All governments can do is reallocate the kind of jobs

★ ★ ★

Smash and Grab

The false notion that government "stimulus programs" can create jobs is called the "broken-window fallacy" in economics, a phrase coined by Henry Hazlitt.[1] Hazlitt illustrated this concept with a story about a hoodlum who throws a brick through a bakery window. Does that create jobs? Well, yes and no, as any good economist would say. What is seen are the jobs "created" in the glass replacement business, but what is not seen is how that money would otherwise have been spent, creating other kinds of jobs elsewhere.

that exist. When the government takes, say, $100 billion out of the pockets of taxpayers and spends it, then yes, there are jobs "created" where all that money is spent. That is what is seen. What is not seen are all the jobs that are destroyed, or that do not materialize in the first place, because all of that money was taken from the citizenry to be spent by politicians and government bureaucrats instead.

Vandalism, hurricanes, earthquakes, and government spending do not create any jobs on net, they only reallocate the kinds of jobs that exist, at best. If government spending in the United States really created jobs on net, there would never be a single unemployed American, so gargantuan is the federal budget. Government "stimulus programs" create the *illusion* of job creation, for which politicians of all parties always take full and immediate credit. But anyone who understands the concept of opportunity cost and the broken-window fallacy will not be fooled by the false "stimulus" rhetoric.

The most famous "stimulus spending" program of all was the Great Depression–era New Deal during the Roosevelt administration. It was a complete bust in terms of job creation, however. According to the U.S. government's own official unemployment statistics, the unemployment rate in 1929, on the eve of the Great Depression, had been 3.2 percent. Unemployment skyrocketed during the Depression, reaching 24.9 percent in 1933. Despite FDR's attempts to get it under control, by 1939, seven years into the New Deal, the unemployment rate was still 17.2 percent. So the unemployment rate was still more than five times higher in 1939 than it was in 1929 (and it declined only to 14.6 percent in 1940).[2] Literally millions of "public works" jobs were "created," but only by severely taxing the sole source of real job creation and destroying private-sector jobs. All the taxes, borrowing, and money-creation that was used to commandeer labor and materials away from the private economy made the Great Depression much *worse* and longer-lasting.[3]

World War II is said to have finally ended the unemployment of the Great Depression, but that, too, is a falsehood. More than ten million men

A Book You're Not Supposed to Read

Burton Folsom, *New Deal or Raw Deal?* (New York: Threshold Editions, 2018).

An analysis of the failures of the New Deal.

were inducted into the army during World War II, so of course there was little unemployment. But there is a difference between a man getting a job, earning income in the marketplace by producing goods and services that improve his fellow citizens' living standards, and being able to return home to his family every night and a man who is conscripted into the army and forced to sit in a frozen hole in northern Europe while bombs rain down on his head.

The real ending of Great Depression unemployment and the explosion of real, genuine job creation occurred only after the war *ended*, the army was mostly demobilized, and federal government spending *fell* from $92.7 billion in 1945, the last year of the war, to $29.7 billion by 1948, a 68 percent decline in federal spending in three years.[4] The positive effect on job creation caused by the ending of the war and the return of all that money to private hands was immediate. As economic historian Robert Higgs wrote, "official data" show "an increase of real nongovernment domestic product [that is, consumption and investment spending] of 29.5 percent from 1945 to 1946."[5] This was the largest one-year expansion of the economy in all of American history. And, of course, the explosion of production was accompanied by the creation of millions of jobs for the soldiers returning from World War II.

The "mainstream" Keynesian economists predicted another Great Depression and massive unemployment after the war; they were dead wrong on both counts, but to this day have refused to acknowledge that reality. They still spread the fairy tale that the massive government spending of World War II ended Great Depression unemployment.

Higher Wages, Better Working Conditions, Shorter Hours, More Products, More Safety

Jobs and improvements in jobs, such as wage increases and better working conditions—shorter hours, more safety—are all products of free enterprise and competition, not government or unions, as so many students of economics are misled into believing. Capitalism cannot grow without capital investment in machinery, tools, equipment, software, and so forth. With more of this kind of investment, the workers themselves also become more productive, creating more goods and services per hour. Education, experience, and on-the-job training ("human capital," in economics lingo) also make workers more productive, but only at a very slow pace, and only in small steps. But with capital investment the increases in productivity are larger and more immediate. Just think of the impact of the invention and use of personal computers, for example.

So employees, without any additional education, experience, or training, are all of a sudden more valuable to employers. Skilled, reliable employees are always in demand, which means that employers are forced by competition to pay their employees more or risk losing them to other businesses. This capital investment by entrepreneurs and capitalists increases the income *of workers*.

In the early days of American capitalism in the nineteenth century, wages grew at approximately a 1.6 percent annual rate from 1820 to 1860, increasing the average worker's paycheck by as much as 90 percent. Between 1860 and 1890, a period known as the "second industrial revolution," real wages (adjusted for inflation) grew by 50 percent in America, while the average workweek shrank.[6] In addition, many new products were invented that made the average working-class person's life even better. The only way for a worker to be paid more while working less is for his productivity to increase so that he produces more per hour. This was primarily the effect of capital investment. In a sense, the American working class has always essentially been a class of free riders on the sacrifices and risk-taking of entrepreneurs and capitalists who stand to lose everything if their investments do not pan out.

A Book You're Not Supposed to Read

Michael Cox and Richard Alm, *Myths of Rich and Poor* (New York: Basic Books, 1999).

Federal Reserve economists prove that the American dream is alive and well, and that complaints about "inequality" rest on mountains of falsehoods.

To put into perspective the effects of capitalist economic growth on the working people of America, economists Michael Cox and Richard Alm explained:

> A nineteenth-century millionaire couldn't grab a cold drink from the refrigerator. He couldn't hop into a smooth-riding automobile for a 70-mile-an-hour trip down an interstate highway to the mountains or seashore. He couldn't call up news, movies, music, and sporting events by touching a remote control's buttons. He couldn't jet north to Toronto, South to Cancun, east to Boston, or west to San Francisco in just a few hours.... He couldn't run over to the mall to buy auto-focus cameras, computer games, mountain bikes, or movies on videotape. He couldn't escape the summer heat in air conditioned comfort. He couldn't check into a hospital for a coronary bypass to cure a failing heart, get a shot of penicillin to ward off infection, or even take an aspirin to relieve a headache.[7]

Economic growth fueled by private enterprise is also responsible for the disappearance of child labor. No one wants children to work in dirty, dangerous factories or at backbreaking, grueling farm labor when they should be in school. Children did work in such situations at one time in America (and still do in other parts of the world), and it was economic growth that allowed their parents to finally take them out of the factories, stop using them as farmhands, and send them to school instead. Higher productivity fueled by capital investment made Americans sufficiently wealthy that child labor was no longer necessary to provide a bare minimum of food for the family and a roof over everyone's head. Governments finally got around to codifying the ending of child labor in law after it had been all but eradicated by capitalist prosperity.

American labor unions that wage anti–child labor campaigns *in foreign countries* are not motivated by compassion but by greed and cruelty. Their goal is to prevent competition from other countries for the products that are produced by unionized American companies—labor market protectionism, in other words. They want to *impoverish* these foreign businesses by blocking them from the American market, causing them to end the employment of children and everyone else. Third World children who work in factories do not have clean, comfortable schools (of the sort that American union executives send their children to) as alternatives. Their alternatives are more likely to be child prostitution, theft, begging, malnutrition, or worse.

It is also economic growth and competition, not government regulation, that has improved workplace safety in America. A dangerous workplace is costly to profit-hungry employers

A Book You're Not Supposed to Read

Morgan Reynolds, *Power and Privilege: Labor Unions in America* (New York: Universe Books, 1984).

Reynolds, a Texas A&M economics professor and the former chief economist at the U.S. Department of Labor, dispels myriad myths and superstitions about American labor unions.

because they must pay what economists call a "compensating difference" in the form of a wage premium in order to attract enough people to work at inherently dangerous jobs such as tuna fishing on the high seas, putting out oil-well fires, welding iron during the building of skyscrapers, and so forth. Consequently, there is money to be made by taking measures to make one's workplace safer. This doesn't guarantee improved safety; there are always fools and derelicts in business, as in all other occupations, who defeat themselves by ignoring safety precautions. But it certainly provides the best possible incentive to improve safety.

And workplace safety has improved immensely. On-the-job deaths declined in America from 428 per million in 1930 to 214 per million in 1960 to less than 40 per million today. Interestingly, this improvement slowed to a crawl and stopped completely for years at precisely the time the federal Occupational Safety and Health Organization (OSHA) was founded in 1970.[8]

Government's Job-Destroying Machinery

Economists have been studying the effects of the federal minimum wage law ever since the first one in 1933. Literally hundreds of studies have found essentially the same result: when governments make it more costly to hire workers with minimum wage laws, employers employ fewer workers.[9] Minimum wage laws cause unemployment. The economics is straightforward. For example, if a fast-food restaurant employs teenagers at, say, $8 an hour, and sells an additional $10 worth of food per hour as a result, the restaurant makes $2 per hour, and the teenagers are employable.

If government raises the minimum wage to, say, $15 an hour, then the restaurant will *lose* $5 per hour, and the teenagers are no longer employable. No business will hire them if it means losing money for every hour they are at work! Only more skilled and experienced (usually older) workers who can help the restaurant make more than $15 an hour will be employable. This has always been the primary effect of minimum wage laws: workers with the least experience and skill—primarily young workers—lose their jobs or won't be hired in the first place, even if other older, more experienced workers benefit.

In 1994 *one* study was published that concluded that increases in minimum wages did not cause higher unemployment. Princeton economists David Card and Alan Krueger surveyed 410 fast-food restaurants in New Jersey and Pennsylvania before and after the 1992 increase in New Jersey's state minimum wage from $4.25 per hour to $5.05 per hour, and claimed that there was no negative effect on New Jersey employment.[10] Politicians and labor unions made instant celebrities out of Card and Krueger and used their study to push for more minimum wage increases. Unfortunately for them (and fortunately for lower-skilled workers), the study has been thoroughly discredited.

A follow-up study by the National Bureau of Economic Research (NBER) found that Card and Krueger collected the data for their study incorrectly, and that the error had tainted their results.[11] They had graduate research assistants conduct telephone interviews with the restaurants in which they asked how many people were working that day. One problem: some workers were there for four hours and others for a full eight hours, but that distinction was not taken into account by Card and Krueger. The NBER study used payroll data from the restaurants, which is more accurate, and then applied the exact same statistical method that Card and Krueger had. The NBER study concluded that, lo and behold, unemployment rose more in New Jersey than in Pennsylvania after New Jersey increased its minimum wage—in keeping with the previous several decades of minimum wage studies. Another study by the Employment Policies Institute found similar results and criticized the "crippling flaws" of the Card-Krueger study.[12]

Labor unions and their supporters in legislatures can be expected to ignore these studies, just as they have ignored hundreds of others for decades that all concluded that minimum wage law increases cause unemployment among the least-skilled and least-educated workers in society. They do so because a higher minimum wage has always been in their financial interest. A simple example can explain why unions—which typically have no minimum wage workers as members—have been the biggest supporters of increases in minimum wages.

Consider a person who is shopping around for someone to paint his house. He finds that he can hire two college students who paint

> ★ ★ ★
> ## That Takes the Prize
>
> In 2021 David Card was a co-recipient of the Nobel Prize in Economics, cited for his methodology of "natural experiments" such as the one comparing employment in New Jersey and Pennsylvania.[13] That was ironic, given that the methodology of that particular study was plagued by "crippling flaws."

houses for tuition money during the summer at, say, $10 an hour each, or an older, experienced, unionized painter who makes $20 per hour. (Because of his superior experience, the unionized painter works twice as fast.)

Then consider what happens if the government raises the minimum wage to $15 an hour. Now, the college students cost $30 per hour compared to the $20 per hour for the union guy. They are priced out of work. That is why unions favor higher minimum wages: they price lower-skilled, non-union competition out of the labor market.

In a study of the political history of minimum wage legislation, economist Thomas Rustici quoted numerous union executives who said exactly this—that they wanted higher minimum wages in order to drive competition for their unionized labor out of the market and into the unemployment rolls.[14] He quotes a Congressman Reuss from Milwaukee saying, "I am proud of the fact that employers in my district have written me asking my support for the $1.25 minimum wage because they do not want sweatshop competition."[15] Notice that he said "employers" wanted a higher minimum wage. It is common for employers and their unions to collude in such efforts to take

A Book You're Not Supposed to Read

Walter E. Williams, *Race and Economics* (Stanford, California: Hoover Institution, 2011).

Professor Williams explains how decades of labor regulation have had the effect of discriminating against African Americans and other minorities.

business (and jobs) away from non-union competitors.

In the early days of the federal minimum wage law, northern-state manufacturers wanted higher minimum wages to handicap competitors in the South that paid lower wages. Rustici quotes Senator Paul Douglas as saying that northern manufacturers wanted "a national scale as a means of protecting themselves against southern competition with lower wages."[16] A Senator Walsh from Massachusetts is quoted as saying that, thanks to a higher minimum wage, "industries in New England...will not continue to be subject to competition...with goods produced by industries that can undersell New England producers...."[17] (Of course, New England *consumers* would then be plundered with higher prices.)

A Congressman Healy from Massachusetts complained that "low-wage areas" have "undermined decent industries [especially textiles] by ruinous competition" from the southern states, which he hoped would be destroyed by the minimum wage.[18] (All to the detriment of his working-class constituents who would then be paying higher prices for textile goods.) Senator John F. Kennedy also complained in 1954 that "New England woolen textile mills pay a wage of at least $1.20 an hour; but...the New England mills must bid for government contracts against southern mills paying only $1.05 an hour."[19] He advocated increases in the federal minimum wage that would have further impoverished Mississippi and other southern-state textile workers by causing them to lose their jobs so that New England textile manufacturers could benefit.

The United States is not the only country where minimum wage laws have been enacted in order to destroy the jobs of relatively low-skilled workers for the benefit of unionized corporations. The South African Economic and Wage Commission of 1925, during the Apartheid era, described the benefit of the South African minimum wage law the following way: "The method would be to fix a minimum rate for an occupation or craft so high that no Native [black workers] would be likely to be employed."[20]

What about Labor Unions?

The main cause of rising American wages over time is increased labor productivity, fueled mostly by capital investment and innovation, along with "human capital" investment—that is, more education, training, and on-the-job experience. At best, labor unions can improve the economic well-being of some of their members but only at the expense of other union members, and especially competing non-union workers.

The effects of unionization on employment are similar to the effects of minimum wage laws, in that if a union successfully increases its members' wages through collective bargaining, *some* unionized workers will be paid more, but *other* unionized workers—usually the last hired and least experienced—will typically be priced out of a job. The new hire who can produce, say, $20 an hour worth of value for the employer is not employable at a union wage of $30 per hour. Older, more experienced union members who can produce $35–40 dollars an hour will benefit from the higher wage.

Private-sector unions can only increase wages above free-market rates, however, by keeping competing non-union labor out. Hence the campaigns for minimum wages and protectionist tariffs and against "child labor" in foreign countries and so forth. As was explained Morgan Reynolds, who served as chief economist of the U.S. Department of Labor:

> A union's problem is painfully obvious: organized strikers must shut down the enterprise, close the market to everyone

else—uncooperative workers, union members, disenchanted former strikers, and employers—in order to force wages and working conditions above free-market rates. If too many individuals defy the strikers…then unionists often resort to force. Unionists ultimately cannot impose noncompetitive wage rates…unless they can prevent employers from hiring consenting adults on terms that are mutually satisfactory. Unions must actively interfere with freedom of trade in labor markets in order to deliver on their promises.[21]

Once again, government-enforced coercion destroys jobs; economic freedom creates them.

CHAPTER 12

The Fed: Government's Boom-and-Bust Machine

The Federal Reserve Board, popularly known as "The Fed," which was created in 1913, is the U.S. government's preeminent central-planning vehicle, since it exerts enormous control over the supply of money in the economy and, in tandem with several other government agencies, regulates almost every aspect of all financial markets. The Fed accomplishes this task by being essentially a legalized counterfeiting operation. In "quantitative easing" or "easy" monetary policy, the Fed purchases billions of dollars of government bonds, putting newly printed cash into circulation in the banking system. It also regulates the "fractional reserve" banking system, in which our banks are required to maintain only very tiny amounts of reserves (sometimes as little as 2–3 percent) as a percentage of all the loans that they are legally allowed make. This is called the "reserve ratio." A bank with, say, $10 million in reserves can lend 50 times that amount, or $500,000,000. Just like that. And when the banks make too many bad loans the Fed—and the U.S. Treasury—bail them out, as they did after the Great Recession of 2008. With bank bailouts, profits are private but losses are socialized. Bankers pocket the profits in good times while you, the taxpayer, cover their losses when their reckless loans go bad.

Remember the capture theory of regulation? The banking industry did not capture the Fed; bankers were the main impetus for its creation back in the early twentieth century. There was nothing to "capture": from its inception the Fed was a cartel-enforcement agency, just as the Interstate Commerce Commission was for the railroad and trucking industries and the Civil Aeronautics Board was for the airline industry. Those two hoary corruption-plagued monopoly machines were eventually stripped of their monopoly-making powers, but not the Fed. So far, anyway.

The Immaculate Conception Theory of the Fed

The political and economic establishments have always pretended that the Fed is the Mother of All Barking Cats: arguably the most powerful of all government agencies, but not influenced in any way by politics, like every other government agency known to man. The Fed is said to be "independent" of politics. Since it is not a greedy, money-grubbing corporation but a government bureaucracy, generations of economics students have been taught that the Fed is managed by selfless public servants who are obsessed with serving only the public interest. Here's what Paul Samuelson's famous textbook taught generations of students about the Fed:

> The Federal Reserve's goals are steady growth in national output and low unemployment. Its sworn enemy is inflation. If aggregate demand is excessive, so that prices are being bid up, the Federal Reserve Board may want to slow the money supply, thereby slowing aggregate demand and output growth. If unemployment is high and business languishing, the Fed may consider increasing the money supply, thereby raising aggregate demand and augmenting output growth. In a nutshell, this is the function of central banking, which is an essential part of macroeconomic management....[1]

So the Fed is supposed to be a kind of technocratic Wizard of Oz that pulls levers, pushes buttons, and creates puffs of smoke to make sure that the U.S. economy is always operating as smoothly as possible in the public interest. Its chairpersons are portrayed as sort of a combination of Mother Teresa and Albert Einstein—or perhaps the maestro of the biggest "orchestra" the world has known. That is the title of a book about former Fed chairman Alan Greenspan: *Maestro: Greenspan's Fed and the American Boom*.[2]

The Fed supposedly has nothing whatsoever to do with propping up the profits of the bankers who lobbied for its creation in the first place and who are its main constituents, defenders, and influencers. Economist Murray Rothbard described "the mythology of the Fed" in the following way:

> **A Book You're Not Supposed to Read**
>
> Murray N. Rothbard, *The Case Against the Fed* (Auburn, Alabama: Mises Institute, 2000).
>
> The former "dean" of the Austrian School of economics makes a case for the abolition of the Fed.

> The public, in the mythology of the Fed and its supporters, is a great beast, continually subject to a lust for inflating the money supply and therefore for subjecting the economy to inflation and its dire consequences. Those dreaded all-too-frequent inconveniences called "elections" subject politicians to these temptations, especially in political institutions such as the House of Representatives who come before the public every two years and are therefore particularly responsive to the public will. The Federal Reserve, on the other hand, guided by monetary experts independent of the public's lust for inflation, stands ready at all times to promote the long-run public interest by manning the battlements in an eternal fight against the Gorgon of inflation. The public, in short,

is in desperate need of absolute control of money by the Federal Reserve to save it from itself and its short-term lusts and temptations.[3]

In reality the Fed has always been a political tool, just like all other government institutions. Only five years after it was created, it was used to finance a large portion of American entry into World War I. Money printing by the Fed, as opposed to direct taxation, made the war *seem* less costly to American taxpayers. There would have been less support for the war—or any other war—if each family was assessed a special war tax of, say, $10,000. The Fed's money-printing causes what some economists call a "fiscal illusion"—government programs seem less costly than they really are. And this is true of all government programs, not just wars.

Economist Robert Weintraub published a historical study in the *Journal of Monetary Economics*, one of the top peer-reviewed economics journals, about how politicized the Fed's behavior was from the 1950s through the 1970s.[4] He showed that when President Eisenhower publicly expressed his wish for slower monetary growth, the Fed complied, with a 1.73 percent annual growth rate of the money supply. When Eisenhower's successor, President Kennedy, advocated faster growth of the money supply, the Fed increased it to 2.3 percent.

When President Lyndon Johnson called for faster monetary growth to finance the Vietnam War and an enlarged welfare state at the same time, the Fed more than doubled the rate of growth to 5 percent annually. These varying monetary growth rates all occurred under the same Fed chairman, William McChesney Martin. His goal was apparently to please the one man with the power to reappoint him to his job (Fed chairpersons serve four-year terms).

Martin's successor, Arthur Burns, was even more of a political animal. As Gerald O'Driscoll, a former vice president of the Federal Reserve Bank of Dallas, explained in the *Wall Street Journal*, "The diary [Burns] kept during the Nixon years confirms that Fed policy became subservient to administration goals and the president's re-election campaign. As he wrote in one entry, he told President Nixon that 'I was looking after monetary policy and he did not need to be concerned about the possibility that the Federal Reserve would starve the economy.'"[5]

When Burns's staff informed him that the money supply was to grow at a robust 10.5 percent annual rate in the months before the 1972 election, he saw to it that it grew even faster. Robert Weintraub wrote that it was the fastest monetary growth of any year since the end of World War II in 1945. And the "great inflation of the 1970s" was the outcome, O'Driscoll explained. (The amount of money in circulation in the economy fuels demand, whereas production is the source of supply. When money supply growth [demand] exceeds supply [GDP] growth, there will be price inflation).

Nixon's successor, President Ford, was stuck with Nixon's inflation and so he wanted slower monetary growth, which was dutifully supplied by Arthur Burns at a 4.7 percent rate, wrote Weintraub. Then Ford's successor, President Carter, irresponsibly called for faster monetary growth to try to salvage his own political future, and the money supply grew at 16.2 percent in just the five months preceding the 1980 presidential election, a repeat of the Nixon gambit. The notion that the Fed is independent of politics is what Murray Rothbard called a fraudulent legend.[6]

With price inflation raging at 13 percent in 1981, the new Fed chairman Paul Volker (appointed by President Carter) accommodated President Reagan's wishes and famously reduced the monetary growth rate drastically, causing a short recession but finally eliminating most of the inflation of the 1970s.

Fast-forward to the Great Recession of 2008, when, as David Stockman, former congressman and director of the U.S. Office of Management and Budget during the Reagan administration, wrote in his book *The Great*

Deformation, what America witnessed was "a capture of the state, especially its central bank, the Federal Reserve, by crony capitalist forces deeply inimical to free markets and democracy."[7]

Stockman described how in the aftermath of the Great Recession the Fed printed nearly twice as much money, primarily to bail out Wall Street investors, in thirteen weeks as it had during the previous century! It was not so much "the economy" that was crashing, he writes, but "the stock prices of Goldman Sachs and the other big banks" such as Morgan Stanley.[8] Morgan Stanley was bailed out after making billions of dollars in bad real estate loans to the tune of $107 billion.[9] After its $10 billion bailout, "Goldman Sachs swiveled on a dime and generated a $29 billion surplus—$16 billion in salary and bonuses on top of $13 billion in net income—for the year that began just three months later."

The insurance company AIG was given a $180 billion bailout gift by the Fed "at a time when 90% of the company's assets were solvent," so that the bailout was "all about protecting the short-term earnings and current-year executive and trader bonuses" and had nothing to do with "saving" the economy, Stockman concluded.[10] In return, the Wall Street investment bankers lavishly finance the careers of Washington politicians of both parties.

The Fed is rewarded very handsomely for doing the political bidding of the Washington establishment. When it prints up money to purchase government bonds, it earns interest on the bonds. Congress places limits on how much of that interest income the Fed can keep and uses that discretion as a political tool to reward the Fed for "good" behavior. A

Government Accountability Office investigation revealed that the Fed has more than twenty-five thousand employees, runs its own air force of more than fifty Lear jets and cargo planes and fleets of vehicles, and has a full-time curator to oversee its collection of paintings and sculptures. The Fed sits on hundreds of billions of dollars in assets and pays quite lavish salaries.[11]

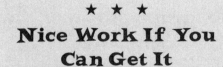

★ ★ ★

Nice Work If You Can Get It

In the 1990s, the head janitor at the Fed was making $163,800 per year in salary and benefits.[12]

More than a Century of Failure

The supposed purpose of the Fed is to "stabilize" the economy by moderating price inflation and unemployment and smoothing out the peaks and troughs of the business cycle. It has failed miserably at this task: there is much evidence and history to show that the Fed has from its beginning in 1913 been a creator of boom-and-bust cycles in the economy, rendering it *more* unstable. To commemorate the centennial of the Fed, economists George Selgin, William Lastrapes, and Lawrence H. White surveyed 195 scholarly economic publications about the performance of the Fed from a historical perspective.[13]

Perhaps the Fed's biggest failure has been in controlling inflation. As the authors of this study concluded: "[The Fed] has allowed the purchasing power of the U.S. dollar…to fall dramatically. A consumer basket [of goods] selling for $100 in 1790 cost only slightly more, at $108, than its [rough] equivalent in 1913. But thereafter the price soared, reaching $2422 in 2008."[14]

Furthermore, the highest annual rates of inflation since the Civil War occurred "under the Fed's watch," they pointed out, referring to the high inflation of 1973–1975 and 1978–1980.[15] (At the time of this writing, in 2022,

★ ★ ★

Oh, Great

During the three decades after the Civil War there was *deflation* in the U.S. economy thanks to the booming industrial revolution and the tremendous increase in production and productivity. Prices fell for decades. This was all for the good, as far as the average American was concerned: being able to obtain more and better products and services at lower prices increases everyone's standard of living. Selgin, Lastrapes, and White conclude, however, that "the Fed has largely succeeded, since the Great Depression, in *eliminating* deflation. . . ."[17] Thanks for nothing, Fed.

the inflation rate in the United States was once again at 1970s levels). All of that inflation is a hidden "tax" on every American's wealth.

Prices also became less predictable after the Fed was created in 1913, compared to previous generations. This makes it harder for businesses and families to plan their expenses. Businesses tend to "sit on their hands" in terms of investments when there is such uncertainty, and that fuels recession.[16]

The authors cite the scholarly work of Christina Romer, President Obama's chief economist and a professor at the University of California at Berkely, showing that the business cycle has been *more volatile* since the creation of the Fred than it was in the decades preceding the Fed's existence. The Fed has caused *de*stabilization, in other words, the opposite of its stated purpose. The volatility of GDP after World War II was actually a third greater than the pre-Fed volatility. Before the Fed was established, recessions were three months shorter, on average, than in the era of the Fed. Thanks a lot, Fed.[18]

Boom-and-Bust Machine

America might never have entered World War I had it not been for the Fed. Created in 1913, the Fed doubled the amount of money in circulation between 1914, the first year of its existence (and the first year of the European War), and 1920. As a result prices, as measured by the Consumer Price Index (CPI), doubled during those years, cutting the value of all privately held wealth in half and depressing real inflation-adjusted wages. Flooding the economy with all that cash created a temporary war-related boom and the inevitable bust, or crash, in 1920. GDP declined by 24 percent from 1920 to 1921, while the number of unemployed Americans more than doubled from 2.1 million to 4.9 million.[19] It was even worse than the first year of the Great Depression a decade later. Thanks a lot, Fed.

The Great Depression of 1920 (that you probably never heard of) lasted only a year. The big reason for this was that the government reacted to the bust with tax cuts, spending cuts, and a generally hands-off policy. American businesses and workers got to work and ended the depression themselves with lots of hard work, entrepreneurship, and perseverance. No wonder the interventionists in the economics profession have kept this a secret, not even mentioning it in their textbooks. To do so would reveal how dubious their knee-jerk calls for more government taxing and spending as the supposed cure for recessions and depressions are.

The Mother of All Fed-Induced Boom and Busts is the Great Depression, which began just nine years (1929) after the Fed had created the bubble that led to the depression of 1920. The "roaring '20s" were indeed roaring economically, with American production of goods and services growing at a very robust level. Normally, this would have resulted in declining prices, with a lower CPI, just as in the late nineteenth century. But the price level remained fairly constant throughout the 1920s, with little or no deflation. The reason for this—in contrast to the falling price level during the "second industrial revolution" of the late nineteenth century—was that in the '20s the newly created Fed increased the money supply in circulation (by 55 percent between July of 1921 and July of 1929). There was an average growth rate of 7.3 percent over those years,[20] which came mostly from greatly expanded loans to businesses at low interest rates, made possible by the Fed's policies. Thousands of American businesses were induced to make excessively risky investments, funded by the banks flush with lendable cash, thanks to the Fed. At some point reality would inevitably sink in: many of those investments were simply not sustainable. That point was reached in October of 1929, with the stock market crash that was the starting gun for the Great Depression.

Up to that point, through all of American history, the response to recessions and depressions (called "panics" up to that time) had been either to do nothing or to cut taxes, tariffs, government spending, and borrowing. This philosophy was perhaps best expressed in 1837 by President Martin Van Buren, who had the misfortune of taking office at the beginning of a recession. Van Buren biographer Major Wilson has called his inaugural address "a charter for inaction" by government.[21] In his first address to Congress, President Van Buren said that "[a]ll communities are apt to look to government for too much" and that "all former attempts on the part of Government to assume the management of domestic or foreign exchange had proved injurious."[22] What was needed, he said, was "a system founded on private interest, enterprise and competition, without the aid of legislative grants or regulations by law."[23]

Historian Jeffrey Hummel wrote that Van Buren "thwarted all attempts to use the economic depression as an excuse for expanding government's role."[24] Federal spending actually fell in absolute dollars during Van Buren's term, from $30.9 million in 1836 to $24.3 million in 1820, a 21 percent decline.[25] He also lowered tariffs on imports and kept America out of any wars. The depression of 1837, like the depression of 1920, ended fairly quickly.

The American government in 1929 was an entirely different creature, thanks to the previous three decades of the Progressive movement, which more or less sought to use government to create heaven on earth.[26] President Herbert Hoover became a conservative after leaving the presidency and made many fine speeches to conservative audiences, but when he became president in 1929 he was a Progressive. He ignored the previous century and a half of American policy on depressions and for the first time in history responded with massive government intervention, which was followed by even more massive government intervention under his successor, Franklin Roosevelt. The result was a fifteen-year-long Great Depression.

Hoover strong-armed American corporations into increasing wages. The higher wages caused even more unemployment, which was exacerbated by the minimum wage law during the FDR administration. Hoover spent 13 percent of the entire federal budget on make-work public programs and raised taxes to pay for it all, draining resources from the pockets of the American working class. He started the policy of paying farmers for not growing crops and raising livestock, in order to increase farm incomes and food prices—another crushing blow to working-class families. He signed the Smoot-Hawley Tariff of 1930, which led to an international trade war that shrank world trade by two-thirds in just three years. And he redirected billions of dollars of bank loans from private investment—the only source of genuine economic recovery—to government boondoggles with his Reconstruction Finance Corporation. Needless to say, none of it worked: the unemployment rate was just a hair under 25 percent in 1933.[27]

FDR's policy was essentially the same, on steroids. His National Recovery Act and Agricultural Administration Act, both of which were ruled unconstitutional by the Supreme Court in 1935, were designed to create hundreds (or thousands) of cartels throughout the entire economy, on the absurd theory that the Great Depression was caused by low wages and prices, and that forcing both up would end it. The government did this with pervasive price floors on manufactured and agricultural goods. But all cartels reduce production levels in order to raise prices. They can't do that without *decreasing* employment levels. Thus FDR made unemployment worse, not better.

The Social Security taxes and unemployment insurance taxes initiated by FDR increased the cost of hiring labor, causing even more unemployment, as did empowering labor unions through union-favorable legislation.

A Book You're Not Supposed to Read

Richard Vedder and Lowell Gallaway, *Out of Work: Unemployment and Government in Twentieth-Century America* (New York: NYU Press, 1997).

Using statistical and historical analysis, Vedder and Gallaway show that the New Deal made the Great Depression more severe and longer lasting.

Wages rose by a phenomenal 13.7 percent during the first three quarters of 1937 alone, causing even more unemployment. Economists Richard Vedder and Lowell Gallaway estimated that the 14.6 percent unemployment rate in 1940 was 8 percentage points higher because of these interventions. On top of all this, federal spending more than doubled from 1933 to 1940, and all that money had to be taken out of the private sector one way or the other. The Hoover and FDR administrations were the high-water mark of "Progressivism," and they created a fifteen-year-long depression.

Fast-forward to the early 2000s. After creating the "dotcom" bubble in the stock market with more excessive money-printing in the 1990s (it burst, causing another recession) and in the aftermath of 9/11, the Fed under Alan Greenspan created more money between 2000 and 2007 than had been created in the entire history of the United States since 1776.[28] An overwhelming amount of this money went into housing because of the federal government's decade-long crusade to make owning a house "affordable" to just about anyone, whether they could really afford it or not.

The Clinton administration and Congress had pressured banks and other institutions to make more mortgage loans to minority and lower-income borrowers, so much so that, with instructions from the Fed, they drastically lowered mortgage loan standards to those groups. An example of what these non-standards were is explained in a Federal Reserve Bank of Boston publication entitled "Closing the Gap: A Guide to Equal Opportunity Lending."

The first thing to do, said the Fed publication, was for banks and all other mortgage lenders to hire more minority employees through affirmative action to enforce the new "standards." Lenders were told to abandon "traditional underwriting standards" such as proof of income when it came to loan applications from minorities and low-income borrowers. Thus was the "no doc" loan invented. The traditional ratios of mortgage payments to monthly income should be dropped, said the Fed, as should the requirement of any credit history—enrolling in a credit-counseling class would suffice. It is illegal for borrowers to switch property appraisers if the first one comes in with an appraisal that might hold up or cancel the loan, but the Fed encouraged lenders to do just that for minority and low-income "sub-prime" borrowers.

In case lenders balked at making billions of dollars in bad loans to unqualified borrowers, the Fed and the Congress assured them that two quasi-government agencies known as Fannie Mae (Federal National Mortgage Association) and Freddie Mac (Federal Home Loan Mortgage Corporation) would buy the bad loans from the lenders on the "secondary market." This eliminated any risk to the primary lenders from making bad or "sub-prime" loans. Apparently one thousand bad mortgage loans to unqualified borrowers with not enough income to make the mortgage payments were bad loans, but bundling them together into a "security" would magically transform them into valuable assets. Everyone knew that if Fannie and Freddie purchased so many of these loans that their solvency was threatened, they would be bailed out by the Fed—and they were.

Then there was the legalized extortion racket known as the Community Reinvestment Act, a Carter administration–era law. This program forced banks to make more loans in "minority" neighborhoods or else face fines or even shutdowns if found guilty of lending discrimination. It created a huge industry of racial hucksters who would essentially blackmail banks into giving them and their organizations, such as ACORN (Association of Community Organizations for Reform Now), Barack Obama's former employer, millions of dollars—as well as extending more loans in minority

A Book You're Not Supposed to Read

Tom Woods, *Meltdown* (Washington, D.C.: Regnery Publishing, 2009).

In his second *New York Times* bestseller, Tom Woods explains why it was the Fed and other government interventions that caused the Great Recession of 2008.

neighborhoods by watering down their lending standards. The watering down of lending standards was promoted and enforced by the Fed, the Department of Housing and Urban Development, Fannie and Freddie, the Congress, and especially President Clinton in the 1990s.

And when the Fed created more money in 7 years than the U.S. government had created in the previous 231 years combined, dropping real mortgage rates to near zero once a little inflation is counted in, hundreds of billions poured into housing, creating the biggest housing market bubble ever. The bubble burst, of course, creating the most severe economic downturn since the Great Depression. Government's boom-and-bust machine had struck again. And the multibillion-dollar bailouts of Goldman Sachs, Fannie and Freddie, and other financial institutions involved in making hundreds of billions in bad loans at the direction of the Fed and other government institutions guarantee that it will happen again. The precedent has been established that there is no risk and all profit involved, a concept that essentially destroys the benefit to society of the allocation of credit and financial capital by private banks.

The political gimmickry orchestrated by the Fed can only persist because the public is, as we have seen, "rationally ignorant." It works marvels for the political class and the banking class (known as "banksters" in some circles), however. During the Fed-created booms, incumbent politicians take credit for the prosperous economy. Then when the bust inevitably occurs they do what politicians always do: they take no responsibility at all for their own actions (in supporting the Fed or forcing lenders to make billions in bad mortgage loans). Instead they blame "greedy bankers," "deregulation," or some other bogey man. They talk as if greed does not exist except in sudden intermittent bursts, when it rears its ugly head to cause a bust, as in 2007. Nor do they ever admit (with one or two exceptions, such as former congressman Ron Paul) that the bank regulatory agencies, including the Fed, have long been in cahoots with the banking industry itself, so that their calls for "more regulation" after the bust occurs are breathtakingly cynical.

A Book You're Not Supposed to Read

Ron Paul, *End the Fed* (New York: Grand Central Publishers, 2015).

The former congressman attracted millions of votes in the 2016 Republican presidential primaries and millions of dollars in unsolicited donations by campaigning on the ideas in this book.

A Defense Orwell Would Be Proud Of

The Fed is a consummate central-planning agency, attempting to fix interest rates (a form of price control), generating boom-and-bust cycles, hiding the true costs of war, generating housing crises, and on and on. It does have its defenders, of course, including some purveyors of Orwellian falsehoods and nonsense. One such defender is business historian John Steele Gordon, who wrote in the *Wall Street Journal* in October of 2008 that the cause of the Great Recession had nothing to do with the Fed's bubble creation or its strong-arming of banks to make hundreds of billions of dollars in bad loans; instead he blamed "the baleful influence of Thomas Jefferson."[29]

Jefferson opposed the creation of the Bank of the United States—a national bank that was a precursor of the Fed—on constitutional grounds. Jefferson's idea that a secret institution shielded from public view that gives politicians control over the entire nation's money supply is a bad idea lives on, said Gordon. There were still critics of the Fed—the most prominent at the time Gordon wrote his article being Congressman Ron Paul. The problem, Gordon claimed, was that—thanks to these critics—the Fed had too *little* power and influence over financial markets, not too much. The Fed was too libertarian, in other words.

This view was echoed in the other big financial newspaper, the *Financial Times*, by stockbroker and Wall Street insider Henry Kaufman. Kaufman argued that Fed chairman Alan Greenspan had been a protégé of Ayn Rand's forty years earlier, and Ayn Rand was an advocate of laissez-faire economics. Therefore, the Fed was by definition a libertarian organization.[30] What ironclad logic!

In reality, as opposed to the opinions of Gordon and Kaufman, the Fed is the exact opposite of a libertarian organization. Over a century of Fed-generated boom-and-bust cycles and the reduction of the value of the dollar by 95 percent were not the result of a "do-nothing" central bank. In addition to destabilizing the economy with its monetary policies, the Fed centrally plans virtually all aspects of all financial markets. A Fed publication entitled "The Federal Reserve System: Purposes and Functions" boasts of the "supervisory and regulatory authority over a wide range of financial institutions" that the Fed possesses, in addition to its money-creating powers. Among those powers are the regulation and "supervision" of these entities:

- Bank holding companies
- State-chartered banks
- Foreign branches of member banks
- Edge and agreement corporations
- U.S. state-licensed branches, agencies, and representative offices of foreign banks
- National banks
- Savings banks
- Nonbank subsidiaries of bank holding companies
- Thrift holding companies
- Financial reporting procedures
- Accounting policies of banks

- Business continuity in case of economic emergencies (i.e., bailouts)
- Consumer protection laws
- Securities dealings of banks
- Information technology used by banks
- Foreign investment by banks
- Foreign lending by banks
- Branch banking
- Bank mergers and acquisitions
- Who may own a bank
- Capital adequacy standards
- Extensions of credit for the purchase of securities
- Equal opportunity lending
- Mortgage disclosure information
- Electronic funds transfers
- Interbank liabilities
- Community Reinvestment Act sub-prime lending demands
- All international banking operations
- Consumer leasing
- Privacy of consumer financial information
- Payments on demand deposits
- Fair credit reporting
- Transactions between member banks and their affiliates
- Truth in lending
- Truth in savings[31]

It is doubtful that the Soviet Politburo ever exercised such comprehensive control over any industry. Thomas Jefferson, the man who said that the natural tendency of things is for liberty to yield and for government to gain ground, would be appalled—but not surprised.

Then there is the Fed's army of academic defenders, a huge percentage of whom have some kind of financial connection to the Fed. It should surprise no one that an institution that has the ability to print money (essentially legalized counterfeiting) can easily afford to employ armies of publicists with Ph.D.s in economics. In 2005, Professor Lawrence H. White of George Mason University published a peer-reviewed scholarly article in which he highlighted the complete dominance of Fed-associated academic economists in the field of monetary economics. He noted that the Fed itself employed 495 full-time economists and engaged more than 120 "leading academic economists" as consultants or visiting scholars.[32] On top of that, it brought 300 or more academic economists to its conferences each year. And you don't need a Ph.D. to understand that being critical of Fed policy would not be a good way to ingratiate yourself with the Fed bureaucracy and procure a seat on the Fed gravy train.

Fully 74 percent of all academic articles on monetary policy published by American economists in that year were either in Fed-published journals or coauthored by Fed economists. Eighty percent of the articles in the *Journal of Monetary Economics*, a top journal in the field, had at least one coauthor with a Fed affiliation. As did 75 percent of the articles in the other top journal in the field, the *Journal of Money, Credit and Banking.*[34]

The Fed is a hoary remnant of the late nineteenth- and early twentieth-century push to create government-sponsored cartels, first in railroads and trucking, airlines, the public utilities, and then for the entire U.S. economy during the New Deal with FDR's National Recovery Act and Agricultural Adjustment Act. The Fed has always operated as a cartel for the benefit of politically connected bankers,

★ ★ ★
They Know What Side Their Bread Is Buttered On

"[I]f you want to advance in the field of monetary research...you would be disinclined to criticize the major employer in the field." —Nobel laureate economist Milton Friedman[33]

and it has truly been a boom-and-bust machine that has destabilized the economy much more often that it has stabilized it. There are alternatives, however.

Nobel laureate economist F. A. Hayek long ago advocated a return to competing currencies issued by private banks—a system of competition, not a government-enforced cartel run by a Wizard-of-Oz-type character (the Fed chairperson).[35] This could be achieved by repealing the Civil War–era legal tender laws that gave the federal government a monopoly in money production, and it would at least subject the Fed to competition.

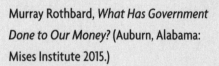

A Book You're Not Supposed to Read

Murray Rothbard, *What Has Government Done to Our Money?* (Auburn, Alabama: Mises Institute 2015.)

A very learned exposition of the origins of money, its evolution on the free market, thousands of years of the gold standard, and the eventual monopolization of money by government central banks.

It would also be possible to require 100 percent reserves, so that banks could no longer lend as much as fifty times or more than what they actually have in reserve, as has been the case for more than a century.[36] The fractional-reserve system has been the root cause of the Fed's boom-and-bust cycles. Placing all of the nation's money in the control of politicians and government bureaucrats in a secretive organization that has such political clout that it has never once been audited was always a horrible idea, as Thomas Jefferson pointed out when his political nemesis, Alexander Hamilton, championed the first national bank, the corruption-plagued Bank of the United States.

CHAPTER 13

The Root of All Evil

As the old saying goes, the only sure things in life are death and taxes. Well, not exactly. When Americans think of taxes, on the top of the list is the federal income tax. But America went for 137 years—from 1776 to 1913—without an income tax, with the exception of a temporary one during the Civil War and for two years during the 1890s until the Supreme Court ruled it to be unconstitutional. In fact, the original constitution prohibited an income tax that is imposed directly on citizens. Article 1, Section 9 of the Constitution states, "No Capitation, or other direct, Tax shall be laid, unless in Proportion to the Census or enumeration herein before directed to be taken."[1] The founders obviously thought that an income tax would be an unmitigated evil. Until the Constitution was amended and a federal income tax was finally adopted in 1913, the main source of federal tax revenue was an indirect tax: tariffs on imports. For 137 years that was sufficient to fund the constitutional functions of government (and then some).

The Lincoln administration was the first to defy the Constitution and adopt an income tax. It started out as a flat tax of 3 percent on all net income above $600 a year and evolved into 5 percent on incomes above $600; 7.5

percent on incomes above $5,000; and 10 percent on incomes above $10,000. There was also a separate 5 percent income tax on interest and dividends.[2] Great resistance to the income tax after the war led to its expiration in 1872.

But politicians, lobbyists, and special-interest groups had tasted the constitutionally forbidden fruit of enriching themselves and advancing their careers by imposing taxes on one group of Americans for the benefit of other, more politically potent Americans. Between 1874 and 1894, sixty-eight bills were introduced in Congress to adopt an income tax.[3] They did temporarily succeed in 1894, with a 2 percent tax on incomes above $4,000, but the Supreme Court ruled it to be an unconstitutional direct tax in 1895.[4]

In terms of economic policy, if the Republican Party (which essentially monopolized national politics from 1861 to 1913) stood for anything, it stood for high protectionist tariffs. Before the Civil War, the average tariff rate in America was around 15 percent. President Lincoln, a career-long protectionist whose official 1861 campaign poster announced, "Protection for Home Industry!," signed ten tariff-increasing bills during his time in office, raising the average rate to the 50 percent range. It would remain roughly at that level or higher for about the next half century of Republican Party dominance.

Protectionist tariffs disproportionately plundered and discriminated against American farmers in the second half of the nineteenth century and into the twentieth century. This is because they exported so much of their produce. At the outbreak of the Civil War, for example, Southern farmers exported about three-fourths of all that they produced, mostly to Europe. Midwestern farmers were in the same boat. So when tariff rates were raised so high as to deter imports, creating domestic monopoly power and monopoly prices, farmers were hit with an unfair double tax.

First, like everyone else, they had to pay more for all the manufactured products (clothing, shoes, farm tools, and hundreds of other items) that had gone up in price thanks to the protectionist tariffs. Second—and this is a little more subtle—the high tariffs that prohibited Europeans from selling their goods in America impoverished them to some degree, so that they were unable to purchase as much American agricultural produce. American farmers did not have to study economics to understand that every time tariff rates were raised, much of their export business dried up. Hence the double taxation: once in higher prices for just about everything at home, and again in terms of lost income from the export business. That is why, in the late nineteenth century, major political pressure to lower tariffs came from America's farmers, who were mostly ignored by the dominant Republican Party, which had always been the party of *corporate* welfare. That all changed once it was understood that the powerful farm vote could assist in getting the Sixteenth Amendment to the Constitution passed to legalize direct taxation with an income tax.

The farmers were promised lower tariff rates in return for their support of an income tax, and so they lent their support. And at the beginning of the Wilson administration in 1913, the average tariff rate was cut about in half from its original position of around 50. Farmers were quite happy, obviously, and not too concerned about the original income tax first-bracket rate of 1 percent on an income of $20,000. That all changed very quickly, however.

While the income tax started out in 1913 with a rate of 1 percent on a $20,000 in income, by 1917 the income threshold was reduced to $2,000. In the next year, the tax rate was increased from 1 percent to 6 percent, with a $4,000 income threshold.

The top rate started out at 7 percent on an income of $500,000, and was paid by relatively few Americans. But by 1917 the top tax rate was raised to a whopping 67 percent, and then to 77 percent a year later. The expansion of the government's tax-collecting bureaucracy led Richard E. Byrd, speaker of the Virginia House of Delegates, to predict that "a hand from Washington will be stretched out and placed on every man's business.... Heavy fines imposed by distant and unfamiliar tribunals will constantly menace the taxpayer. An army of Federal officials, spies, and detectives will descend upon the state. . . ."[5] Truer words were never spoken.

In the post–World War I years, the top income tax rate was reduced to 25 percent by 1928, but on an income threshold of $100,000.[6] But by 1930, President Hoover and the Republicans had raised the top income tax rate to 63 percent. And Hoover's successor, FDR, increased it all the way to 94 percent by 1945. Not until 1964 was the top rate lowered to 77 percent. It was finally reduced substantially, to 28 percent, in the Reagan tax-rate cuts of the early 1980s.

Meanwhile, the farmers of America (and everyone else) soon realized that they had been swindled once again by the slick politicians in Washington. The 1922 Fordney-McCumber Tariff increased tariff rates by 138 percent in just two years.[7] By the mid-1920s the average tariff rate was near 40 percent, leaving farmers (and everyone else) with high tariffs *and* much higher rates of income taxation than they had been misled into believing would be the case.

The Root of All Evil?

"Old Right" conservative literary icon Frank Chodorov subtitled his book *The Income Tax* "Root of All Evil."[8] That may appear to be a bit over the top, but he made a powerful case that the income tax should be at least in the top ten. His initial point was that the Constitution was designed to keep the federal government, which was delegated only a dozen and a half or so specific powers by the sovereign states, "off balance and weak."[9] A weak federal government is the corollary of a strong people, said Chodorov. The income tax amendment destroyed all of that by:

- Enabling the federal government to put its hands in everyone's pockets

- Drawing the public's allegiance away from local governments and to Washington instead
- Causing citizens to have less control over faraway federal representatives, as opposed to local mayors and town councils and governors
- Making citizens subject to the whims of federal politicians
- Causing the state governments to lose their autonomy and their independence
- Causing state and local governments to become subservient to the politicians and bureaucrats in Washington
- Enabling the federal government to bribe and threaten state governments, forcing them to bend to its will
- Destroying the system of federalism established by the Constitution and replacing it with a consolidated, monopolistic, highly centralized government, the opposite of the intentions of the founders

Americans were literally turned into slaves of the state, said Chodorov, for what the government was now saying to its citizens was: "Your earnings are not exclusively your own. We have a claim on them, and our claim precedes yours. We will allow you to keep some of it, because we recognize your need, but not your right; but whatever we grant you for yourself is for us to decide.… The amount of your earnings that you may retain for yourself is determined by the needs of the government, and you have nothing to say about it."[10]

In other words, the income tax was the biggest attack on the principle of private property in American history. That is why the founding generation—and the next several generations—so strongly opposed the idea of direct taxation of incomes.

It may sound shocking to the average American's ears, but Chodorov was right when he argued that all socialists, beginning with Karl Marx, had

★ ★ ★

Corrupting the Public

Early twentieth-century humorist Will Rogers is said to have remarked that "the income tax has made more liars out of Americans than golf has." Like all good comedy, there is more than a grain of truth in that. The way that the much less humorous Frank Chodorov put it was: "The income tax, by attacking the dignity of the individual at every base, has led to the practice of perjury, fraud, deception, and bribery. Avoidance or evasion of the levies has become the great American game, and talents of the highest order are employed in the effort to save something from the clutches of the State. People who in their private lives are above reproach still resort to the meanest devices to effect some saving and will even brag of their ingenuity. The necessity of trying to get along with the income tax has made us a corrupt people."[14]

advocated income taxation precisely because it went such a long way toward their primary goal of the abolition of private property. In their famous "Ten Planks" of *The Communist Manifesto*, Marx and Engels listed "Abolition of Private Property" as their top, number one priority. The second plank was "A Heavy Progressive or Graduated Income Tax."[11] The second plank has always been the Marxist roadmap to the first plank. In today's America, "Tax Freedom Day" occurs each year in late April. The day is calculated by dividing all taxes paid by all national income, to get the percentage of income that goes to taxes. This means that the average working American works almost one-third of the entire year just to pay taxes, more than he or she works for food, clothing, and shelter combined.[12] And, as Chodorov perceptively wrote, although "we long ago abolished debtors' prisons, we do have prisons for those who violate the income tax laws."[13]

A Book You're Not Supposed to Read

Frank Chodorov, *The Income Tax: Root of All Evil* (Greenwich, Connecticut: Devin-Adair, 1974).

The "Old Right" icon speaks truth to power about the income tax.

In his classic *Freedom and Federalism*, Felix Morley wrote that the income tax amendment was "an attack on the remnants of State Sovereignty" because "it openly bypassed the entire structure of the States to bring the full coercive power of central government to bear continuously on their citizens."[15] It essentially turned most state governments into puppets of the "federal" government once the federal government had enough funds with which to bribe or threaten the states to bend to its will by either granting or withholding "aid to the states."

Most states (along with some cities and towns) eventually adopted income taxes of their own, which led to the further centralization of government. State governments also play the game of threatening to withdraw state "aid" if local governments do not behave as the state politicians wish.

A Book You're Not Supposed to Read

Felix Morley, *Freedom and Federalism* (Chicago: H. Regnery Co., 1959).

The best book ever written about American federalism, including a discussion of how destructive income taxation is to this cherished and uniquely American institution.

The Real Burden of the Income Tax

How much income taxes actually cost us is not so easy to determine as simply looking at IRS data on tax payments. Like all taxes, the income tax causes changes in various kinds of economic behavior, which in turn affect the economic well-being of more people than just those who pay the taxes. The national Taxpayers Union compiles and publishes IRS statistics on who pays federal income taxes every year. In a recent year the top 10 percent of income earners ($145,135 and above) paid 70.8 percent of all income taxes. The top 1 percent of income earners ($515,371 and above) paid 38.47 percent of income taxes. The bottom 50 percent of all income earners in America with an income of $41,740 or less paid 3.11 percent of income taxes. This breakdown is likely to be similar with state income taxes. Income taxation in America is extremely "progressive."[16]

The U.S. income tax is obviously very discriminatory against more productive, higher-income earners. The harder one works, the more successful is one's business, the more popular is the product or service that one provides, the more one is penalized by the tax system with higher rates of taxation. This is called "progressivity"—or "fairness." It is said to be more "fair" for the government to take from the more productive people in society and give to the able-bodied unproductive in the form of welfare and other income-transfer programs.

This phenomenon was on display in 2020–2022 when federal unemployment insurance payments were increased, along with the length of time one could collect unemployment insurance, causing labor shortages everywhere, especially in the restaurant business. Millions of able-bodied people were apparently paid more (or close to the same) to just stay at home and collect unemployment checks instead of going to work.

As of 2022 there are seven different federal income tax "brackets" (10, 12, 22, 24, 32, 35, and 37 percent), guaranteeing that all income earners will be appropriately punished for doing a better job of supporting themselves and their families. In 1980 there were sixteen federal income tax brackets. A single taxpayer with an annual income of $23,500 faced a 39 percent federal income tax rate, which jumped up to 49 percent at an income of $34,100, showing how quickly one could be pushed up into a much higher bracket.[17] The income tax was not indexed for inflation at the time, so that several years of inflation could push taxpayers into significantly higher tax brackets even though their real income after adjusting for inflation had actually fallen. That was remedied by the Reagan tax cuts that by 1986 reduced the brackets to just four (11, 15, 28, and 35 percent). Indexing was also achieved at that time.

The main rationale for "progressive" income taxation ever since Abraham Lincoln first introduced it to America is the so-called "ability to pay" principle: the idea that those with a greater ability to pay should pay *proportionately* more. Of course, if equality rather than ability to pay were the primary philosophy of income taxation then everyone would pay *the same percentage rate*. With a 10 percent flat income tax, for example, a person with, say, $30,000 in income would pay $3,000 in tax, whereas a person with ten times more income—$300,000—would pay $30,000, that is, ten times more tax. With today's "progressive" income tax that person would be in the 35 percent bracket and owe $105,000. (Deductions and exemptions are ignored here to make the principle simpler to understand). A flat or proportional income tax is still discriminatory, but a little less discriminatory than a "progressive" income tax.

"Progressive" taxation is supposed to be justified by the "ability to pay" principle—which, in reality, is arbitrary, nonsensical, and impossible to enforce in a fair manner. Consider two taxpayers with $50,000 in income each. The "ability to pay" principle says that they have an equal ability to pay. But what if one of them has $250,000 in savings and the other has none? Do they still have an equal ability to pay? Or what if one has five children and the other has none? Or if one taxpayer has extremely high medical bills that are not covered by insurance? Complications like these make it impossible to come up with any sensible definition of "ability to pay." When it comes down to it, the real reason for supporting progressive income taxation is envy, one of the seven deadly sins, no matter how many fanciful alternative theories are invented by economists and others to try to salve their consciences over their support for governmental plunder of their fellow citizens.[18] As for the bureaucrats and the politicians, they want to tax higher-income individuals at higher rates for the same reason that bank robbers rob banks: that's where the money is.

Economic Destruction

When income tax rates become high enough, they create a disincentive to work. In 1980 a single taxpayer with $108,300 in taxable income was in the 70 percent tax bracket. That means that once he or she earned that much, the federal government would take $700 for every additional $1,000 in income. Millions of educated professionals, business owners, and others in that income category decided to quit working altogether several months before the end of the year, spent large amounts of money on tax accountants and tax attorneys to legally evade taxes, or cheated on their taxes. This was one of the key reasons why Ronald Regan was elected president in 1980—he promised to cut tax *rates* (and reduce the number of tax brackets) with a promise of *increasing* tax *revenue* by increasing the work incentive and reducing the incentive to evade or cheat on taxes. It worked: federal tax revenues approximately doubled from $517 billion in 1980 to over $1 trillion by 1990. This was even a 28 percent increase in real tax revenue after adjusting for inflation.[19]

A more subtle negative effect of income taxation on the economy is that people save less as well as consume less when they pay more in taxes. Savings is what fuels capital investment, the prerequisite for economic growth. Income taxation causes savings to be scarcer, which also makes interest rates rise to a higher level than they otherwise would be (the supply and demand for credit is a main ingredient of interest rates). Less capital investment makes labor less productive and therefore more poorly paid.

New or improved capital and technology make labor more productive. As a simple example, think of how much more productive farm workers became after the invention of the gas-powered tractor, compared to walking behind a plow and a mule all day long. So when there is less capital investment there will be slower labor productivity growth and slower wage growth as well. The entire country's standard of living is harmed. The "cost" of the income tax is not just the amount of money that is sent to Washington, D.C., from working peoples' bank accounts.

More Tax Loopholes, Please

It seems that just about everyone—especially everyone in Washington, D.C.—criticizes "tax loopholes," or legal deductions that only some individuals and businesses qualify for. The loopholes come and go as tax laws change, but there have been thousands of them over the years. "Mainstream" economists tend to be critical of loopholes—and of anyone who lobbies for more loopholes. Their argument is that all the time, effort, and money that is spent learning about loopholes, hiring tax accountants, and so forth is socially wasteful. Without the loopholes, they say, more people would just go to work and be more productive. They call the loopholes, and the energy devoted to creating and taking advantage of the loopholes, a "deadweight loss" to society because none of it results directly in any good or service being produced.

But the underlying premise of this argument is that the government has taken too little from the pockets of taxpayers, and that society as a whole would be better off if taxpayers were poorer and government bureaucracies richer. Private individuals always spend their own money more efficiently (to fulfill their own needs) than politicians and bureaucrats do, however. Handing over more of your hard-earned money for government bureaucrats to spend is anything but "efficient."

An alternative way of looking at all the time and resources spent taking advantage of tax loopholes is that it is an investment in being able to keep, spend, and save one's own money. From that perspective, tax accountants and lawyers who are loophole experts are providing a most valuable service to families, businesses, and civil society in general by keeping more funds out of the greedy clutches of the already-bloated-beyond-belief Washington bureaucracy. As economist Ludwig von Mises once said, tax loopholes allow capitalism to "breathe."[20] Then there's the argument of "unfairness." Loopholes should not be permitted, the reasoning goes, unless everyone can benefit from them. So why not advocate that more people be allowed to benefit from them? But instead, "mainstream" economists use the disparity to argue that no one should benefit. This is similar to another of their favorite arguments: that if only some industries are given tax breaks, more resources will flow to those industries, and that is inefficient or artificial compared to a genuinely free market with no special tax favors to anyone. This sounds reasonable, but it ignores the central question, namely, what is the alternative? If tax credits going to a few industries are ended, the result will be more tax revenue being collected by government and spent by the bureaucracy rather than being reinvested in those industries (or other industries). Why is that necessarily a good thing? We need *more* tax loopholes, not fewer.

The early twentieth-century jurist Oliver Wendell Holmes famously quipped that taxes are "the price we pay for civilized society." If that were true, then the Soviet Union, Nazi Germany, Eastern Europe during the Cold War, and today's North Korea would be the most "civilized" nations in history. In fact, the opposite is more likely to be true. As renowned investor and author Doug Casey has written,

> Taxes are destroyers of civilization and society. They impoverish the average man. They support welfare programs that anchor the lower classes at the bottom of society. They underwrite a gigantic bureaucracy that serves only to raise costs and quash incentive. They pay for public works programs...that are usually ten times more costly than their privately-funded counterparts, whether needed or not. They maintain programs that

cause huge distortions in our economy.... And they foster a climate of fear and dishonesty. The list of evils goes on. But the simple truth is that anything needed or wanted by society would be provided by profit-seeking entrepreneurs, if only the tax collector would retire.[21]

Every word of that is true.

CHAPTER 14

"Trade Agreements" Are Not Free Trade

The case for free international trade is essentially the same as the case for free, voluntary exchange between any two people in any country. The voluntary exchange of goods and services for money is mutually advantageous—it benefits both parties *as they see it*. This is true whether the trade takes place between two Americans, or an American and a Canadian, or any other parties.

International trade expands the division of labor in the world and makes all participating countries more prosperous. As we saw in chapter 1, it is the division of labor that makes human civilization as we know it possible: we all specialize in some task in our work lives, earn money by doing it, and purchase all the necessities and non-necessities of life from others who specialize in other things. That's why the poorest of the poor can live a decent life—and look to myriad opportunities to better themselves—in a capitalist economy with a high degree of economic freedom. The hordes of immigrants risking life and limb to get into the United States obviously understand this, even if they have never opened an economics book!

Free international trade expands the size of markets for businesses, and those larger markets in turn provide them with opportunities to achieve

★ ★ ★
Take Your Pick
The nineteenth-century French economic writer and statesman Frederic Bastiat is known for the slogan, "If goods can't cross borders, armies will."

economies of scale from larger-scale production. This typically leads to lower prices as they become ever more competitive internationally, to the benefit of consumers.

Free international trade also encourages peaceful relations among people from different nations and cultures. Familiarity breeds peace. So does the recognition that doing business with people from other countries can make you richer and more prosperous. For centuries scholars have recognized that free international trade can be a powerful deterrent to war. Thomas Paine wrote in his famous book *Common Sense* that "[a] foreign policy based on commerce [that is, free trade] would secure for America the peace and friendship of the Continent [of Europe] and allow her to shake hands with the world—and trade in any market."[1] Paine also believed that free international trade would "temper the human mind" and help people "to know and understand each other," having a "civilizing effect" on everyone involved.[2] George Washington apparently agreed. In his Farewell Address he said that our commercial policy "should hold an equal and impartial hand; neither seeking nor granting exclusive favors or preferences; consulting the natural course of things; diffusing and diversifying by gentle means the streams of commerce, but forcing nothing."[3]

It is not a stretch to say that the opposite of free trade—autarky, or producing everything within a single country with no trade—was a major cause of World War II (and of many other wars before it). Autarky was the economic policy of Nazi Germany. The Nazis soon discovered, however, that Germany did not have nearly the resources necessary to prosper without international trade. Their solution was to invade and conquer other countries to steal *their* resources, a reversion back to feudalism, from an economic perspective.

Nations that mutually prosper by trading with each other are not inclined to kill the goose that lays the golden eggs. It was believed in the Middle Ages and even before that that the way to accumulate wealth was through war, conquest, and theft. Capitalism changed all of that, and international trade is simply capitalism squared. People learned, in other words, that they can prosper by *serving* their fellow man instead of enslaving or killing him—and it is much less risky, since most people are strongly inclined to oppose being enslaved or killed.

Free international trade is just common sense, for a number of reasons, including what is called "absolute advantage." For example, America has plentiful farmland and can produce agricultural crops as cheaply as anyone. Saudi Arabia, on the other hand, has very little arable land, but is rich in petroleum. America's absolute advantage is in agriculture, and Saudi Arabia's is in petroleum. We sell the Saudis food that they cannot provide for themselves as economically as we can, and we buy petroleum from them, sometimes for cheaper than the cost of drilling for it in the United States, as Saudi Arabia and other Middle Eastern oil-producing countries were blessed with plentiful oil relatively close to the earth's surface, making it cheaper to extract.

Even if one country can produce *everything* at less cost than another country, it still pays to trade for some things—on the principle of "comparative advantage": it still makes sense for people to specialize in their best skills—in producing their most remunerative products—and to trade with others, whether at home or abroad, for other things. Consider an individual (as opposed to country-to-country trade) example. Imagine a lawyer who bills clients at $100 per hour and is also a champion typist, having taken typing class in elementary school and typed his school term paper and other writing assignments all through high school, college, and law school. He can type two hundred words a minute, mistake-free.

A Book You're Not Supposed to Read

Pierre Lemieux, *What's Wrong with Protectionism* (London: Rowman and Littlefield, 2018).

Addresses all of the main protectionist superstitions.

The lawyer employs an assistant whom he pays $25 an hour and who types legal documents at 100 words per minute, mistake free. There is a typing job that will take the assistant four hours, and the lawyer two hours to complete. Who should do the typing job at the law firm?

To answer this question, we must compare the cost of the lawyer doing the typing to the cost of the assistant doing it. After all, this is a for-profit law firm, and the lower the costs the higher the profits. Two hours of typing will cost the law firm $200 since the lawyer could have used that time lawyering and billing a client at $100 per hour. Four hours of typing by the assistant will cost the law firm only $100 (4 hours at $25 per hour). Thus, even though the lawyer has a comparative advantage over the assistant at both lawyering and typing, it pays to have the assistant do the typing job. The same reasoning applies when talking about individuals in one country who can produce everything more cheaply than those in another country.

Free trade is just a synonym for competition. Competition produces lower prices and forces businesses to strive to improve the quality of their products and services, to pay competitive wages and salaries lest they lose their best employees, to invent new and better products and services as a matter of survival in a global economy, and generally to enrich communities. Protectionism, or government-imposed restrictions on international trade, has the opposite effects.

Protectionism: Protecting Consumers from Low Prices

One of the ironies of the Trump administration was that while President Trump was indeed a populist (that's why the Washington establishment hated him so much), at the same time he advocated the most anti-populist of policies, protectionism. In terms of international trade, he was not a populist but as establishmentarian as anyone.

The main tools of protectionism are tariffs—essentially a sales taxes on imported products—and quotas, which are numerical limits on how many units of a product may legally be sold in the United States. In early America, before the 1913 income tax, the average tariff rate waxed and waned between what was called a "revenue tariff" and a protectionist tariff. The former was usually around 10 or 15 percent. The idea was that a tariff in that range was high enough to raise sufficient revenue to fund the constitutional functions of government, but not so high as to significantly deter competition from abroad.

A protectionist tariff in the range of 50 percent, such as was ushered in by the Lincoln administration, is intended to block imports from abroad. With protectionist tariffs or quotas, supply on the market is restricted, consumers have less to choose from, and they will pay higher prices for the same product or service (which will eventually decline in quality as well). Unlike normal free-market exchange, with tariffs consumers simply pay more and get nothing in return. It is not a positive-sum game but a zero-sum game of robbing Peter (consumers) to pay Paul ("protected" industries). Thus, what citizens are protected from with protectionist tariffs and quotas is lower prices and better-quality goods spurred on by more competition, more product innovation, and more prosperity in general.

Protectionism is always a matter of collusion between businesses (and often their unions) and government to provide financial benefits to a relatively small, concentrated group at the expense of everyone else (who must pay higher prices for the "protected" items). It is crony capitalism and anti-populism at its worst. As Frederic Bastiat said, it is legalized plunder. The only real difference between robbery with a gun and protectionism is the gun. In each instance coercion is used to take money from one person only to give it to another, totally undeserving, person.

For generations, the lobbyists and publicists who work for corporations and unions seeking protectionist tariffs and quotas have invented myriad myths, superstitions, and economic falsehoods with which they try to bamboozle a rationally ignorant public into thinking that higher prices are in the public's best interest. Chief among them is the "Buy American" scam designed to make people believe that protectionism will somehow save American jobs. The truth is that protectionism may temporarily preserve some jobs in the protected industry, but always at the expense of destroying other American jobs elsewhere and plundering American consumers with higher prices. A clear example would be tariffs on steel, which have been in place since the nineteenth century. By pushing up the price of steel, the tariffs make everything made of steel more expensive. The American automobile industry incurs higher costs that make it less competitive on world markets, meaning that it employs fewer workers than it otherwise would. All thanks to the higher prices caused by the tariffs on steel. The same is true for everything else made of steel. And that's just one item among hundreds that may have tariffs applied to them.

Another centuries-old red herring argument is that imports disturb the sacred "balance of trade" between imports and exports. This is a remnant of the seventeenth- and eighteenth-century theory known as "mercantilism." Mercantilists believed that paying for imports with gold would deplete a country of gold and impoverish it. That didn't happen, but the theory lives on with "economic nationalists" who always condemn the "trade deficit" when imports exceed exports.

But the "trade deficit" is merely a statistical artifact. It is no more alarming than the fact that every family most likely has a trade deficit with the local grocery store. To this day, your author has yet to sell a single book or lecture to any grocery store in America, despite spending thousands of dollars in such establishments every year. What is wrong, anyway, with receiving valued products from other countries (great cars from Japan, great wine from France, lumber from Canada, delicious coffee from Brazil, and so forth) in return for pieces of paper (dollars)?

When there is a trade deficit and more dollars leave the United States than come into the United States to purchase exports, those dollars eventually make it back to the United States one way or the other anyway. People in other countries buy American goods and services with them, go on vacation, invest in the American stock market, purchase American land and real estate, or put money in American banks for the purpose of financing business transactions, for example.

Protectionists complain when too much money is supposedly leaving the country with the purchase of imports. And then they turn around and complain that too much money is coming *into* the country in the form of foreign investment, making us a "debtor nation." But when people in other countries invest in America instead of their own country, that is a good thing for America, not a bad thing. It means they have more confidence in the economic future of America than in their own country; otherwise they would have invested at home instead.

The United States was a "debtor nation" all throughout the late nineteenth century during the "second industrial revolution" because foreigners had more optimism about the U.S. economy than they did about their own countries. This is a sign of economic strength, not weakness.

Then there is the child labor complaint: that certain countries that use child labor should not be permitted to export goods into the United States. Labor unions are especially prolific with this argument, pretending to be so concerned about the well-being not of their own members, but of children in Third World countries.

All around the world it was prosperity created by the growth of capitalism that ended child labor. No one wants his children to work in fields and factories instead of going to school—unless the survival of the family is at stake. As soon as economic conditions permitted, children disappeared from fields and factories. If the United States prohibits imports from a Third World country because of child labor, it will be economically harmful to that country, causing more poverty there and therefore *more* child labor, not less. Unions couldn't care less about these children; they crusade against "child labor" as part of their lobbying campaign for protectionism for the benefit of their own dues-paying members *at the expense* of children in the Third World.

Just as sure as the sun rises in the East and sets in the West, whenever foreign companies succeed at underpricing American companies (for cars, steel, or whatever), there will be complaints from protectionist businesses and unions about "dumping." The legal definition of "dumping" is selling something in the United States at a lower price than the price at which it is sold at in the home country. Anti-dumping laws once again "protect" Americans from lower prices.

Dumping is just the international version of the myth of predatory pricing—the theory that the lower prices are part of a diabolical James Bond–ish plot to drive all of the American businesses in an entire industry into bankruptcy, after which the sky will be the limit as far as prices are concerned. This has never happened in the real world, and for good reason. As we saw in chapter 2, only a fool would believe that such a scheme could be successful. The idea nevertheless appeals to a segment of the rationally ignorant public, which is why such claims are so often made during protectionist lobbying campaigns.

Perhaps the most hypocritical protectionist argument is that, in the name of "fair trade," imports should be banned from countries whose governments subsidize certain industries. The U.S. government is hardly sinless in that regard. It subsidizes American corporations with its Export-Import Bank, among other institutions, for example. And besides, what's wrong with foreign aid in reverse? If the Japanese government wants to reduce your next set of car payments by subsidizing the Japanese car industry, that's not necessarily a bad thing.

Nor is protectionism necessary for national defense purposes, as has been argued for generations. A wartime army is an entire civilization in itself, and military personnel need everything that everyone else needs to live, in addition to all of their armaments, weapons, and equipment. This means that once the argument is accepted that products needed for national defense should be isolated from international competition, then just about everything is fair game. It makes a case for autarky, in other words.

Military readiness is much better served by a *competitive* economy, not one in which competition is blocked every step along the way. It is competition—not monopoly via protectionism—that spurs on innovation, product improvement, and cost-cutting. Capitalism, including free trade—not the economic sclerosis of government-mandated monopoly power—is the best route to a stronger military.[4]

Trade Agreements Are NOT Free Trade

There have been many multi-country "trade agreements" over the years, the best-known of which (to Americans, anyway) is the North American Free Trade Agreement (NAFTA) of 1994, the treaty between the United States, Canada, and Mexico, from which President Trump wisely withdrew the United States after a quarter of a century. NAFTA is a prime example of how things that politicians call "free trade agreements" are never anything of the sort. A genuine free trade agreement simply abolishes tariffs and quotas and other hindrances to free trade. Neither NAFTA nor any other multi-country "trade agreement" does that.

Just because politicians call something a "free trade agreement" doesn't make it one. They always choose wonderful-sounding names for their legislation, which in reality is usually the work of scores of greedy, plunder-seeking lobbyists. That was the case with NAFTA, which was some 2,400 pages of bureaucratic regulation and central planning of the trade between the United States, Canada, and Mexico and the rest of the world. It contained nine hundred pages of tariffs, the opposite of free trade. As Mises Institute president Lew Rockwell wrote at the time in the *Los Angeles Times*, "Maybe that's why the treaty is available for public viewing only a few hours a week, by appointment, in a room full of cranky clerks who resent mere citizens interrupting their…conversations."[5]

The protectionist nature of NAFTA was illustrated by one bureaucratic edict that required "high tariffs" on all cars that were not at least "62.5% North-American Made"—discriminating against Japanese, German, Swedish, South Korean, and other imports.[6] Politicians only promised lower tariffs on some items *fifteen years into the future*, when many of them, as far as they knew, would be retired and not in a position to legislate anything. It was a classic "I'll gladly pay you Tuesday for a hamburger today" scam akin to the old *Popeye* cartoon character Wimpy. (In the cartoon, Tuesday never came.)[7] What else should one expect from a 2,400-page law "written by a cabal of lawyers from government and big business"?[8]

NAFTA also created a gigantic new bloated supranational government bureaucracy to "manage" North American commerce. That sounds more like Soviet central planning than free trade. Free trade does not need to be centrally planned by thousands of international bureaucrats. Such a bureaucracy was ripe for bribery and manipulation of trade and tariff policy by all kinds of protectionist special interests. It is a wonder that anyone was fooled by the "free trade" language of NAFTA, for its proponents were often forthright about its purposes. President Clinton himself proclaimed that one of its purposes was to keep "more products from Japan and Europe" from being imported "into America."[9] James Sheehan of the Competitive Enterprise Institute studied NAFTA for years and concluded that "NAFTA did not live up to its billing—many trade barriers remain, while still others were raised. NAFTA's first two years [were] characterized by the typical hallmarks of excessive government: mercantilist planning, environmental controls, industrial policy subsidies, and bailout guarantees. The treaty did not simply lower tariff barriers between member countries, it erected new barriers to outside parties and created a new bureaucracy capable of entangling trade policy in a morass of environmental and social concerns. . . ."[10]

It is a bit ironic that on the one hand President Trump championed protectionism—made protectionism a major campaign promise, and increased tariffs—but on the other hand he championed freer trade by withdrawing from the protectionist NAFTA. His dealmaker's instinct was right when it told him to denounce NAFTA as one of the worst trade deals ever, although his economic instincts were dead wrong when he thought that protectionist tariffs were the route to overall American prosperity. The former was, ironically, good economics; the latter was not only bad economics but dangerous to peace and prosperity.

Socialism
(Or How to Destroy an Economy, Impoverish People, and Deprive Them of Their Freedoms)

In 1989, in the midst of the worldwide implosion of socialism, the socialist economist Robert Heilbroner authored an article in the left-wing *New Yorker* magazine entitled "The Triumph of Capitalism."[1] Heilbroner held the Norman Thomas Professorship of Economics at the New School for Social Research, named after the early twentieth-century Socialist Party presidential candidate, and his article was a *mea culpa*. After advocating socialism for some fifty years, Heilbroner finally admitted that "Mises was right" about socialism all along. He was referring to Ludwig von Mises, author of the monumental book *Socialism* and the most famous critic of all forms of socialism in the first half of the twentieth century.[2] Mises had explained why socialism could never be a viable economic system and that it would only produce extreme poverty, misery, and chaos. That is exactly what it did in dozens of countries over many decades, all over the world, from Albania to Venezuela and beyond. The people suffered horribly (and died prematurely by the millions) while the ruling classes lived high on the hog by exploiting the working classes with subsistence wages and prohibiting them from improving themselves through economic freedom.

Socialism was originally defined as government ownership of the means of production, as in the old Soviet Union. The definition evolved, however, so that by the 1970s it came to mean the pursuit of "equality" with the institutions of progressive income taxation (the Second Plank in *The Communist Manifesto*) and the welfare state, according to F. A. Hayek.[3]

As we have seen, Mises—who was Hayek's intellectual mentor—wrote in his book *Socialism* that socialists everywhere have always been "destructionists" first and foremost, meaning that they always intend to first destroy as many institutions of existing society as possible. Only then do they think about replacing them. In Mises's day the instruments of "destructionism" included the nationalization of industries as well as onerous taxation, excessive government regulation of industry, the welfare state, inflation, and whatever other government interventions could be used to destroy capitalism piece by piece.

Socialism "is not... the pioneer of a better and finer world," wrote Mises, but "the spoiler of what thousands of years of civilization have created. It does not build; it destroys; for destruction is the essence of it. It produces nothing, it only consumes what the social order based on private ownership in the means of production has created." It is "the policy of the spendthrift who dissipates his inheritance regardless of the future."[4]

This exact scenario has played out in socialist country after socialist country. The Soviets lived off the capital that had been accumulated by previous generations (and that which they confiscated from other countries that they invaded). "Fabian" socialism after World War II in Britain consumed capital until the economy ground to a halt with the "British disease" of the 1970s, a phrase that was used to describe the dysfunctionality of Britain's socialistic, nationalized industries.

Capitalist Sweden was one of the most prosperous countries in the world in the late nineteenth and early twentieth centuries, until it adopted a version of socialism in the 1950s. The result was that not one single new job was created on net in Sweden in the ensuing fifty-five years; interest rates reached 500 percent in the 1980s; and there have been attempts to de-socialize ever since.[5] More recently, the once-prosperous Venezuelan economy was destroyed in less than a decade after Hugo Chavez, the latest in a long line of Castro admirers serving as president of Venezuela, nationalized virtually all of industry and imposed universal price controls. A country that is said to have more oil than Saudi Arabia suddenly saw formerly upper-middle-class

A Book You're Not Supposed to Read

Thomas DiLorenzo, *The Problem with Socialism* (Washington, D.C.: Regnery Publishing, 2016).

A handbook explaining why socialism of any kind should be avoided like the plague, because it is in fact a plague on humanity.

people searching through garbage in the streets looking for food and killing zoo animals for meat.[6]

Mises wrote that for Karl Marx and his socialist followers, "all politics was only the continuation of war by other means.... The socialist parties...who have taken the Marxist parties for their model have elaborated the technique of agitation, the cadging for votes and for souls, the stirring up of electoral excitement, the street demonstrations, and the terrorism."[7] This sounds very familiar in the wake of the months of rioting, looting, and arson in American cities in 2020 by self-described socialist terrorist organizations Antifa and Black Lives Matter, whose founders proudly announced that they are "trained Marxists."[8]

Although Mises was writing in the early 1920s, he described what today is known as "fake news." He wrote that "the literati" were essentially "recruiting agents for socialism" who were "paving the way for destructionism." This certainly sounds like today's "mainstream media."

Nor are today's attacks on Western civilization—religion, the traditional family, the rule of law, capitalism, constitutionalism, tradition, and the like—anything new. Mises quoted various socialists who "have hailed with

★ ★ ★
First Things First

As Ludwig von Mises pointed out, all socialists are first and foremost "destructionists." Before they can have their socialist utopia, they must first destroy economic freedom, religion, the family, and Western civilization itself with its "oppressive" rule of law, respect for property rights, protections of individual liberty, tolerance, constitutionalism, freedom of speech, freedom of religion and assembly, and, most of all, consent of the governed.

great enthusiasm...writings which call for the destruction of all cultural values...."[9]

There are several very fundamental economic reasons why socialism is economic poison wherever it is tried. First, there is the so-called incentive problem. If everyone is supposed to have equal income regardless of effort, talent, habits, bodily strength, or anything else, then people will quickly discover that the person who does not work at all will be given the same income by the state as the hardest and most conscientious worker. If there is no link between effort and reward, the workers will think of themselves as chumps for working, and so will reduce or stop their efforts altogether.

This was widely understood, including by the Russian socialists who experimented for decades with comical, failed schemes (and mind-boggling propaganda) to stimulate incentives. As economist Murray Rothbard explained:

> [E]veryone, socialists and non-socialists alike, had long realized that socialism suffered from an incentive problem. If, for example, everyone under socialism were to receive an equal income, or, in another variant, everyone was supposed to produce "according to his ability" but received "according to his needs," then, to sum it up in the famous question: Who, under socialism, will take out the garbage? That is, what will be the incentive to do the grubby jobs, and, furthermore, to do them well? Or, to put it another way, what would be the incentive to work hard and be productive at *any* job?[10]

It would be as though a college professor announced that every student in the class was to receive the average grade of "C" regardless of how anyone performed on any exams or term papers. How much effort would *you* put into such a class?

A more serious problem stems from the absence of private property and thus of the prices determined by supply and demand in free markets. The biggest part of this problem was that under socialism no one could have any idea how to organize production in an efficient manner in terms of cost because there would be no way of knowing what "capital goods"—things used to produce the final products that we buy at the stores—cost. Automobiles, for example, contain literally several thousand different parts, and there are myriad substitutes for almost all of them. Even windshields come in all different types and qualities of glass. Automobile producers decide which parts to use primarily based on prices determined in markets. Without market prices, why not use gold or platinum instead of aluminum? For the extra safety-conscious, why not six-inch steel all around, kind of like a tank? If both steel and gasoline prices are arbitrarily fixed by government bureaucrats at low levels, why not? That was the reality in the socialist economies of the Soviet empire, communist China, Cuba, North Korea, and elsewhere.

A third reason why socialism is always and everywhere economic poison is what F. A. Hayek called "the knowledge problem." In his last book he labeled it "the fatal conceit."[11] The point here is that in order for an economy to operate successfully there must be a vast decentralization of knowledge. Scientific knowledge is valuable, but just as valuable, if not more so, is all of the

A Book You're Not Supposed to Read

Yuri Maltsev, ed. *Requiem for Marx* (Auburn, Alabama: Mises Institute, 1993).

A Soviet defector who worked for Mikhail Gorbachev and became an American citizen and an economics professor edited this volume of essays, which drives very large nails into the coffin of Marxism.

knowledge in the minds of the millions of working people who perform all of the essential tasks required to produce and market all the essentials (and non-essentials) of life. No one mind or group of government "experts," even if equipped with the most powerful computer in the world, could ever replicate all of that information and utilize it in a rational way. The fatal conceit of socialism is that government bureaucrats supposedly *can* do that. History and reality proved them to be dead wrong.

"Equity": The Mask of Totalitarianism

In the Soviet Union socialist central planning immediately caused what Mises predicted it would: the near total destruction of the nation's economy, with untold numbers of people literally dropping dead from starvation. This in the one nation on earth with more natural resources than any other. But the socialists never gave up on their utopian fantasy—with its primary goal always being "equality," or as today's socialists prefer to call it, "equity." What this really means, and has always meant, is the complete stamping out of human diversity and individuality with the heavy hand of government coercion, intimidation, and violence. But, as Murray Rothbard explained, "The Left, of course, does not couch its demands in terms of stamping out diversity; what it seeks to achieve sounds semantically far more pleasant: *equality*. It is in the name of equality that the Left seeks all manner of measures, from progressive taxation to the ultimate stage of communism."[12]

The ultimate purpose of socialism has always been the creation of a totalitarian

★ ★ ★

Participation Trophies for Everyone!

If "it takes a village" to raise a child, and the "village" is government, you can be assured that "the village" will do everything imaginable to destroy the individualism of children and indoctrinate them in the alleged evils of high achievement.

★ ★ ★

Literary Critiques

The great twentieth-century social critic H. L. Mencken explained that as even democratic governments become more socialistic, one of their "primary functions" is "to regiment men by force, to make them as much alike as possible…to search out and combat originality among men. All it can see in an original idea is potential change, and hence an invasion of its prerogatives. The most dangerous man to any government is any man who is able to think things out for himself, without regard to the prevailing superstitions and taboos."[13] In "Harrison Bergeron" Kurt Vonnegut Jr. lampooned socialist egalitarianism:

> The year was 2081, and everyone was finally equal. They weren't only equal before God and the law. They were equal in every which way. Nobody was smarter than anybody else. Nobody was better looking than anyone else. Nobody was stronger or quicker than anybody else. All this equality was due to the 211th, 212th, and 213th Amendments to the Constitution, and to the unceasing vigilance of agents of the United States Handicapper General.

For example,

> [T]he ballerinas…weren't really very good—no better than anybody else would have been, anyway. They were burdened with sashweights and bags of birdshot, and their faces were masked, so that no one, seeing a free and graceful gesture or a pretty face, would feel like something the cat drug in.[14]

When prominent literary figures like Kurt Vonnegut and H. L. Mencken portray socialist egalitarianism in this way, one comes to understand how deeply hateful of humanity it is. Perhaps such intense hatred of God's creations explains why so many socialist governments in history have been atheistic, and why so many socialists, Karl Marx the first among them, have been atheists who seem to wage perpetual political war on religion.

government that will enforce uniformity or "equity" in all aspects of life, erasing God's work and creating a new master race designed in the socialists' image. That is what "equity, inclusion, and diversity"—the endlessly repeated mating call of the contemporary socialist—really means. Socialists mean to *exclude* by force, if necessary, anyone who does not comply with their central plan for society, and to *stamp out human diversity* as much as possible. It is a war against human nature that can only be fought with totalitarian governmental powers. As Rothbard explained, socialists have "a deep-seated hatred of individual diversity" as well as "a hatred for the intellect and its works, since the flowering of reason and intellection leads to diversity and inequality of individual achievement."[15]

The traditional American notion of "equality under the law" is in inherent conflict with the notion of socialistic "equity." The former principle, also known as "the rule of law," means that everyone is to be treated the same way by the law, no matter who they are or what their background or situation in life is. A billionaire is the equal of a homeless person before the law. Race and ethnicity do not matter either.

With socialism's compulsion to redirect and redistribute income and all other resources in its quixotic pursuit of "equity," it must necessarily treat different people, and different groups of people, *differently*, not equally. Taxing one person only to give the money to someone else who did nothing at all to earn the money is not treating people equally. Neither is the whole apparatus of government regulation with its price ceilings and floors and controls—every one of which benefits one (usually much smaller) group at the expense of another (typically much larger) group of citizens. "Any policy aiming directly at a substantive ideal of distributive justice," Hayek wrote, "must lead to the destruction of the rule of law."[16]

Fascism *Is* Socialism

The Nazis were National Socialists. That's what the word "Nazi" meant. They were proud members of the National Socialist German Workers' Party. The same is true of the Italian "fascists" of the early twentieth century. Fascism is merely a variety of socialism. From an economic perspective, the difference between the Russian socialism and German socialism (that is, fascism) of the twentieth century is that the Russians nationalized virtually all industry, whereas the German socialists nationalized about half of German industry and then severely and comprehensively regulated, regimented, and controlled the rest. Although that half of the German economy remained "privately" owned, it was forced to produce only what the state approved of and wanted it to produce; to employ only the workers that the state permitted it to employ (No Jews Need Apply); and to charge state-approved prices. It was *de facto* socialism, in other words, but it was still socialism.

F. A. Hayek wrote about how Nazi Party policies were thoroughly anti-capitalist and socialistic, with "a fierce hatred of anything capitalistic" and a "violent anti-capitalistic attack." The Nazis portrayed the Jews as symbols of hated capitalism.[17] An early Nazi slogan and "accepted dogma" (in the Nazis' own phrase) was "the End of Capitalism."[18]

This is why it is so bizarre that in today's world there are self-described socialists and communists (Antifa) who claim to be "anti-fascist," when in fact the real fascists of the twentieth century were the ideological blood brothers (and sisters) of all other socialists everywhere. They were all birds of a socialist feather. As F. A. Hayek wrote, "The various kinds of collectivism, communism, fascism, etc. differ among themselves in the nature of

A Book You're Not Supposed to Read

Lew Rockwell, *Fascism versus Capitalism* (Auburn, Alabama: Mises Institute, 1993).

The founder of the Mises Institute describes our fascist American economy and makes the case for a return to capitalism.

★ ★ ★ Distinction without a Difference?

The Nazis (National Socialists German Workers' Party) distinguished themselves from the *international* socialists in Russia by calling themselves *national* socialists. Communists and Nazis were ideological blood brothers, nonetheless.

A Book You're Not Supposed to Read

F. A. Hayek, *The Road to Serfdom* (Chicago: University of Chicago Press, 1976).

There was a long prison sentence awaiting anyone caught with this book in the Soviet Union, so fearful were the communists of its ideas. And they still are—particularly the communists at Google, Instagram, Facebook, and so forth.

the goal toward which they want to direct the efforts of society," but they all want to "organize the whole of society and all its resources for this unitary end.... In short, they are totalitarian in the true sense of this...word...."[19]

Socialism means government *control* of the means of production, if not outright ownership. The twentieth-century fascists understood that they would be at least a little more prosperous if they allowed *some* profit-seeking incentives in their economy (albeit closely watched over and regulated by the state). Or at least that they would be better at producing armaments than their fellow socialists in Russia. Either way, government control of a nation's economy is a recipe for totalitarian tyranny, for if government can control where you work, what you do for a living, how much income you are allowed, where you spend your money, and the like, then it can control your entire life, and you have precious little freedom left. "An authority directing the whole economic system would be the most powerful monopolist conceivable," wrote Hayek, and "economic planning [by government] would involve direction of almost the whole of our life."[20]

It takes a certain kind of person to be a socialist central planner who suffers the fatal conceit of thinking that he or she can somehow direct an entire society. As we have seen, the inherent failures of socialism mean that it is bound to produce poverty and economic dysfunction—as it has done whenever it has been tried throughout history. Politicians, whether in a dictatorship or a democracy, are loath to admit their mistakes, so the usual response to the failures of socialism is to double down on the same things: more government coercion, more controls and regulations, more taxes, and less freedom. The politicians will be forced "to choose between disregard of ordinary morals and failure," and "[i]t is for this reason that the unscrupulous and uninhibited are likely to be more successful" in such a regime, said Hayek.[21] Those with the fewest qualms about stripping their fellow citizens of their freedoms and even using violence against them will rise to the top in such a regime.

The failures of socialism typically give rise to the popularity of a strongman with dictatorial powers who will "get things done"—not through legislation but through "executive orders" and other dictates. It is telling that the U.S. government now has more than one hundred presidential appointees known as "czars" who are given executive powers, often without being confirmed by Congress for the job. They are given dictatorial powers, in other words. Did you know there is a weatherization czar, an Asian carp czar, and a reading czar, as well as, more ominously, a war czar, terrorism czar, COVID czar, and AIDS czar?

Historically, socialism has been associated with dictatorial government, although sometimes a façade of "democracy" is maintained. Maintaining power requires a large number of supporters, and Hayek categorized them: First are the least-independent thinkers, who will take orders. Then come "the docile and gullible" who, without any system of values of their own, "are prepared to accept a ready-made system of values if it is only drummed into their ears sufficiently loudly and frequently."[22]

It is also typical for the state to instigate hatred of a "common enemy," since "it is easier for people to agree on a negative program...than on any positive task."[23] "German anti-Semitism and anti-capitalism spring from the same root," wrote Hayek, since the Nazis viewed the Jews as symbols of the evils of capitalism. (Your author writes this as "the unvaccinated" are being mercilessly demonized by the highest reaches of the U.S. government and its supporting cast in the media, with some even calling for them to be imprisoned, fired from their jobs, kicked out of schools, denied medical care, and essentially banished from society).

Truth itself is always a casualty of socialist economic planning, for the whole apparatus depends on a long series of what Hayek called "official myths" about the altruism and effectiveness of the state and the evils of capitalism and the civil society. "The whole apparatus for spreading knowledge—the schools and the press, radio and motion picture—will be used exclusively to spread those views which, whether true or false, will strengthen the belief in the rightness of the decisions taken by the authority; and all information that might cause doubt or hesitation will be withheld."[24] This sounds a lot like American society today, with pervasive censorship by schools, the media, and especially Big Tech.

As Hayek pointed out, "the disinterested search for truth cannot be allowed" because it might interfere with the "official myths" that are the bedrock of the state's power. The word "truth" itself, said Hayek, "ceases to have its old meaning" and "becomes something to be laid down by authority...in the interest of the unity of the organized effort" of socialist state planning.[25] Such "unity" is a periodic campaign theme of American presidential candidates, despite the fact that the very notion of unity is absurd and ridiculous in a nation of several hundred million people. (One suspects that it is easier to claim "unity" of opinion about experimental vaccines, for example, because those who question them and refuse them can be kicked off social media platforms by Big Tech—and out of their jobs by the government—for doing so).

Finally, "intolerance, too, is openly extolled." In Hayek's time that meant "persecution of men of science and the burning of scientific books," among other atrocities. In today's America it means "hate speech" laws, university censorship of conservatives, the demonization of doctors and scientists who question the pronouncements of the federal Centers for Disease Control or the Food and Drug Administration, and the elimination of thousands of ordinary people (and quite a few doctors and medical researchers) who are skeptical of various governmental pronouncements about "public" health from social media platforms. No second opinions are permitted when it comes to "public health" as they are with private health care. Medical "truth"—now known as "the science"—is discovered solely by the pronouncements of government bureaucrats.

You're Killing Me! Socialized Medicine, Anyone?

In democratic as well as non-democratic countries, socialism begins and ends with a mountain of Big Lies. The biggest lie is that socialism can magically provide goods or services for free. That explains the popularity of lifelong socialist Senator Bernie Sanders with teenagers and college students: promising something for nothing will always appeal to the naïve and uneducated. "Free" public schools, "free" public libraries, "free" college, and "free" cell phones all fall into the Big Lie category, but the biggest lie of all is that medical care can somehow be "free"—if only government is given a monopoly over it.

But doctors, nurses, medical technicians, hospital administrators, and the thousands of other employees who work in hospitals and doctors' offices are not slaves, and they do not work for "free." (Even if they *were* slaves, it would still cost a lot to feed, clothe, and house them!) MRI machines, X-ray technology, and all other medical technology is not free, either. What deceitful politicians like Senator Sanders really mean when they bloviate about how medical care is a "right" that should be "free" to everyone is that: 1) medical care should be provided only by government bureaucrats after the government grants itself an ironclad monopoly; and 2) the costs of medical care should be hidden in general taxation, or paid for (in an equally hidden way) by government borrowing and inflationary money-printing by the Fed.

Common sense suggests that medical care will always be orders of magnitude *more* expensive under a government-run monopoly than under a competitive, free-enterprise system, even if a large part of the public is

★ ★ ★

Halfway There

A large part of medical care in the United States is already socialized, with Medicare and Medicaid and the federal Veterans Administration bureaucracy. The rest is arguably the most heavily regulated of all industries.

duped by the Santa Claus–ian political promises of "free" medical care. Such a system would, as the old saying goes, have all the efficiency of the Department of Motor Vehicles and all the compassion of the IRS.

Great Britain and Canada nationalized their medical care decades ago, and it is not uncommon to hear clueless Canadians visiting America boasting of how inexpensive their medical care is! (Your author heard this hundreds of times from vacationing Canadians while living in Florida).

The economics of socialized medicine, euphemistically called "the National Health Service" by the British and Canadians, is fairly straightforward. By making medical care "free," or offering it for a nominal payment at the point of service, with everything else covered by tax dollars, the *perceived* price is zero or close to zero. This will inevitably cause an explosion of demand; everyone wants as much as possible of just about anything that is perceived to be free. Doctors will have an incentive to prescribe unlimited "tests" even when they know they are unnecessary because, hey, they're "free" to the patient. The cost of everything and anything related to medical care goes through the roof. Senator Phil Gramm, a Ph.D. economist who taught at Texas A&M University before becoming a United States senator, was only slightly exaggerating when, in the debates over socialized medicine during the Clinton administration, he proclaimed that there's not enough money in the world to pay for it.

To cover up the explosion of medical care costs caused by socialization, politicians in Great Britain, Canada, the United States, and elsewhere have imposed price ceilings on everything from doctors' visits and salaries to hospital room rates and technology charges. As we saw in chapter 2, price controls inevitably cause shortages: the supply of doctors, nurses, hospitals, and medical technology can never keep up with the skyrocketing increases in demand triggered by the artificially low price of medical care. The price controls also cause a "brain drain," whereby doctors and other medical care professionals who have spent many years in school before becoming qualified in their professions leave countries with partially or wholly socialized medicine for less socialistic countries. For decades, the United States benefited from many highly talented medical professionals who had left the United Kingdom and Canada. American hospitals have also benefited from all the Canadians who, unable or unwilling to wait months or years for needed medical procedures in the shortage-plagued Canadian medical care system, traveled to the United States for treatment and spent their medical dollars here. Only the more affluent Canadians can afford to do this; lower-income Canadians are stuck waiting (or dying while they wait for treatment).

Medical care shortages under socialism manifest themselves in the form of months- or years-long waiting times for sometimes urgently needed medical procedures. Canadian patients wait eight weeks on average to see a specialist, and then another nine and a half weeks before treatment, including surgery. In New Zealand the average time for elderly patients waiting painfully for needed knee- or hip-replacement surgery is between 300 and 400 days. Some New Zealanders wait more than two years for surgery.[26]

An investigation by a British newspaper found that delays in treatment of colon cancer patients by the National Health Service were so long that 20 percent of the cases were "incurable" by the time the patients finally saw

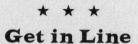

★ ★ ★
Get in Line

In Britain more than a million people are waiting to be admitted to a hospital on any one day; in Canada one survey found that 876,000 people were waiting for treatments; in socialized-medicine Norway more than 270,000 people wait daily for medical treatment; and in New Zealand some 90,000 people wait on any given day.[27]

a specialist. They found similar results for lung cancer and cardiac patients.[28] An internet search for "hospital shortages in Canada" revealed that the Canadian government is constantly warning the public about shortages of medical care, particularly in nursing, drugs, hospital beds, medicine, and doctors.[29] As is so often the case when governments interfere in the free market, the more affluent fare better under socialized medicine than the poor do. As the British newspaper *The Guardian* explained, with the National Health Service, "[g]enerally speaking, the poorer you are the more socially deprived your area, the worse your care and access is likely to be."[30] A British "Good Hospital Guide" found that hospitals in wealthier parts of London had four times the number of doctors per hundred patients than there were in the poorer sections of the city.[31]

The Soviets were the founding fathers of socialized medical care, as the Soviet Union was the first country to provide "cradle-to-grave" government-monopoly medical care. The Soviets sounded a lot like Bernie Sanders (or vice versa) when they proclaimed "a right to health" and "health care for all." Professor Yuri Maltsev, an economics professor at Carthage College in Wisconsin who served as an advisor to Mikhail Gorbachev, defected from the Soviet Union, and became a U.S. citizen, wrote that after seven decades of socialized medicine in the U.S.S.R., "healthcare institutions in Russia were at least a hundred years behind the average U.S. level."[32] He described Russian hospitals just before the collapse of the Soviet Union as characterized by "filth, odors, cats roaming the halls, drunken medical personnel, and absence of soap and cleaning supplies."[33] The Soviet government once admitted, said Professor Maltsev, that 80 percent of AIDS patients had contracted the disease from dirty needles in state-run hospitals.

Professor Maltsev, whose sister is a physician, said that neurosurgeons in the Soviet Union were paid one-third of what bus drivers were paid, which would not be the way to attract the best and brightest to the field of neurosurgery. Bribery was rampant, as it always is whenever government-set prices or outright socialism cause shortages. Patients had to pay bribes to receive anesthesia before surgery and were routinely shown the door just before dying so that the hospital's death statistics would not look so bad.

There was no hot running water in 57 percent of Russian hospitals, and hospitals in rural areas often did not have water or sewage treatment at all. As in other socialist countries, the political elite did not participate in the squalor and dysfunction of the hospitals that ordinary citizens had to endure. They had special hospitals for themselves or, unlike the average citizen, could fly off anywhere in the world for treatment. Moreover, there is nothing uniquely Russian about any of this, according to Professor Maltsev: "It is a direct result of the government monopoly on healthcare and it can happen in any country.... Socialized medical systems have not served to raise general health or living standards anywhere. In fact, both analytical reasoning and empirical evidence point to the opposite conclusion. But the dismal failure of socialized medicine to raise peoples' health and longevity has not affected its appeal for politicians, administrators, and their intellectual servants in search of absolute power and control."[34]

The last thing in the world anyone should want to put government in charge of is health.

Epilogue

In his 1949 treatise *Human Action*, legendary economist Ludwig von Mises explained how political bias had already infected and compromised much of the field of economics. "Tax-supported universities are under the sway of the party in power," he wrote, where "[t]he authorities try to appoint only professors who are ready to advance the ideas of which they themselves approve."[1] This is truer today than ever.

By 1949 all non-socialist governments, Mises wrote, were "firmly committed" to government interventionism, and "appoint[ed] only interventionists" as professors.[2] The "first duty of the university" was therefore "to sell the official social philosophy to the rising generation." As such, "they [had] no use for economists."[3] They had no use for economists because economic common sense so easily allows one to understand the foolishness and danger of their socialistic and utopian fantasies. Nevertheless, because of this powerful bias, "The majority of the students espouse[d] without any inhibitions the interventionist panaceas recommended by their professors."[4]

Yours truly was always amazed at how so many undergraduate college students just could not grasp the logic of the simplest and most elementary economic concepts, such as the laws of supply and demand or the principle of opportunity cost, but could at any moment present an hour-long oration about recycling, global warming, the "living wage," or whatever other left-wing fads and superstitions were fashionable at the time—topics that had apparently been drilled into their heads since preschool.

For decades students of economics (and all other students for that matter) have been subjected to classroom recitations of leftist slogans and catch-phrases instead of being taught how to think independently for them-selves—what used to be the hallmark of a college education.

F. A. Hayek once argued that political bias is bound to be the strongest in the fields of history, law, and economics, for those are the disciplines that are most involved with social policy. Consequently, for many of today's college graduates, their degrees are mere proof that they successfully mem-orized all the right politically correct slogans, theories, and catchphrases. No wonder Mises said in 1949 that by then most universities had already become "nurseries for socialism."[5]

Thankfully, this phenomenon has never been universal. There has always been a remnant of teachers *and their students* who have intellectually armed themselves as defenders of economic freedom. After all, as Mises also pointed out, there are many young people "who are keen enough to see through the fallacies of interventionism."[6] This, too, has been my experience as a university professor. As just one anecdotal example, recall our discus-sion of the Fed and how it has failed to control inflation, has made business cycles *more severe*, and has also failed to moderate unemployment. I once had a junior-year economics major in a class say to me, "I had no idea that criticisms of the Fed existed, and I've taken all the courses offered by the economics department on the subject." Economics education wasn't always so biased; many of us were taught that there were indeed debates about Fed policy, but that has apparently changed in today's politically correct campus environment.

As you can tell from the broad array of topics discussed in this book, economics is not just about making money, organizing industrial production, and understanding the latest GDP or unemployment statistics. Mises believed that understanding how markets work—and how governments *don't*—is a matter of understanding "the philosophy of human life and action and concerns everything and everybody."[7] Why else would virtually all the governments in the world do everything possible to monopolize economic education with the goal of teaching only the politically correct economic ideas to the next generation?

While other academic disciplines are even further down the road to politically correct hell, too much of economic education teaches the "evils" of economic freedom, free trade, private property, and peaceful, voluntary exchange (a.k.a. "market failure"), while demanding intervention by supposedly wise, benevolent, and selfless public servants and their experts (and ignoring pervasive government failure).

The danger is that "blind reliance upon 'experts' and uncritical acceptance of popular catchwords and prejudices" is tantamount to the abandonment of self-determination, wrote Mises. One is submitting to be dominated and politically controlled by others, in other words.[8] Thus it is therefore all of our *civic duty,* according to Mises, to familiarize ourselves with the teachings of economics.

My purpose in writing this book has been to stimulate interest in doing just that—and to help you, dear reader, to become your own economist, to continue learning long after you have put this book down, and to pass these habits along to family, friends, and fellow citizens in general. It is not a stretch to argue that what tyrants fear the most is not insurrectionists or revolutionaries but sound economic ideas. Economic common sense is a powerful weapon—arguably *the most powerful* weapon—in defense of a free and prosperous society.

Notes

Introduction

1. Doug Casey, "How Economic Witch Doctors Convince Everyone They're Neurosurgeons," Lew Rockwell, December 2021, https://www.lewrockwell.com/2021/12/dodug-casey/how-economic-witch-doctors-convince-everyone-tyere-neurosurgeons/.

2. Ibid.

3. These quotations from the founding document of the AEA are from Bernard Weisberger and Marshall Steinbaum, "Economists of the World, Unite!," *Democracy Journal* 40 (Spring 2016), https://democracyjournal.org/magazine/40/economists-of-the-world-unite/.

4. Murray N. Rothbard, "Origins of the Welfare State in America," Mises Institute, https://cdn.mises.org/12_2_1_0.pdf.

5. William Peterson, "A History of the Mont Pelerin Society," *The Freeman*, July 1, 1996, https://fee.org/articles/a-history-of-the-mont-pelerin-society/.

Chapter 1: What Is "the Free Market," Anyway?

1. Burton Folsom, *The Myth of the Robber Barons: A New Look at the Rise of Big Business in America* (Herndon, Virginia: Young America's Foundation, 2018).

2. Adam Smith, *An Inquiry into the Nature and Causes of the Wealth of Nations* (New York: Random House, 1937), 422.

3. misesmedia, "What Is Morally Right about Economic Freedom—Daniel Lapin," YouTube, March 20, 2009, https://www.youtube.com/watch?v=lVS0vIkTrsw.

4. Zaw Thia Tun, "8 Most Successful Products from 'Shark Tank,'" Investopedia, November 10, 2020, https://www.investopedia.com/articles/investing/082415/10-most-successful-products-shark-tank.asp.

5. U.S. Constitution, Article 1, Section 8, Yale Law School website, https://avalon.law.yale.edu/18th_century/art1.asp.

6. Ludwig von Mises, *Socialism: An Economic and Sociological Analysis* (Auburn, Alabama: Mises Institute, 2011).

7. Ludwig von Mises, *Human Action: A Treatise on Economics* (Auburn, Alabama: Mises Institute, 1988), 270.

Chapter 2: The Worst Economic Idea in the World

1. Ludwig von Mises, *Socialism: An Economic and Sociological Analysis* (Auburn, Alabama: Mises Institute, 2011), Part 5, "Destructionism," 457–500.

2. Fred S. McChesney, *Money for Nothing: Politics, Rent Extraction, and Political Extortion* (Cambridge, Massachusetts: Harvard University Press, 1997).

3. Ludwig von Mises, "Middle-of-the-Road Policy Leads to Socialism," Mises Institute, December 2, 2006, https://mises.org/library/middle-road-policy-leads-socialism/midroad.asp.

4. "Celebrities Love New York Rent Control," Frontier Centre for Public Policy, December 19, 2005, https://fcpp.org/2005/12/19/celebrities-love-new-york-rent-control/.

5. John T. Flynn, *The Roosevelt Myth* (New York: Devin-Adair, 1948), 45.

6. *A.L.A. Schechter Poultry Corp. v. United States,* 295 U.S. 495 (1935).

7. Frederic Bastiat, *The Law*, excerpts available at the Mises Institute website, https://mises.org/library/law/html, 8.

8. *Munn vs. Illinois* 94 U.S. 113 (1876).

9. James Madison, *The Federalist* no. 10, available at Library of Congress website, https://guides.loc.gov/federalist-papers/text-1-10 #s-lg-box-wrapper-25493273.

10. Ibid.

11. Robert Schuettinger and Eamon Butler, *Forty Centuries of Wage and Price Controls* (Auburn, Alabama: Mises Institute, 2014).

12. Ibid, 10.

13. Ibid, 11.

14. Ibid.

15. Schuettinger and Butler, *Forty Centuries of Wage and Price Controls.*

16. Ibid, 41.

17. Ibid.

18. Ibid., 47.

19. Lawrence Reed, "Ludwig Erhard: Architect of a Miracle," *The Freeman*, May 7, 2015, https://fee.org/articles/lemonade-from-le mons/; David Henderson, "German Economic Miracle," Econlib, https://econlib.org/library/Enc/GermanEconomicMiracle.html.

20. Schuettinger and Butler, *Forty Centuries of Wage and Price Controls*, 73.

21. "Crude Oil Prices," MacroTrends, https://www.macrotrends.net/13 69/crude-oil-price-history-chart.

22. Alfred Kahn, *The Economics of Regulation: Principles and Institutions* (Cambridge, Massachusetts: MIT Press, 1988).

Chapter 3: The Nirvana Fallacy in Economics (Or, How to Attack a Straw-Man Argument)

1. Thomas DiLorenzo and Jack C. High, "Antitrust and Competition, Historically Contemplated," *Economic Inquiry* 26, no. 3 (July 1988): 423–35.

2. Bryan Caplan, "Why Were American Econ Textbooks So Pro-Soviet?" Econlib, December 29, 2009, https://www.econlib.org/arc hives/2009/12/why_were_americ.html.

3. Ibid.

4. John Kenneth Galbraith, *The Affluent Society* (New York: Mariner, 1998); John Kenneth Galbraith, *The New Industrial State* (Princeton, New Jersey: Princeton University Press, 2007).

5. Joan Robinson, *The Economics of Imperfect Competition* (New York: Palgrave, 1969); Edward Chamberlin, *The Theory of Monopolistic Competition* (Cambridge: Harvard University Press, 1965).

6. Harold Demsetz, "Information and Efficiency: Another Viewpoint," *Journal of Law and Economics* 12, no. 1 (April 1969): 1–22.

7. F. A. Hayek, "The Meaning of Competition," in F. A. Hayek, *Individualism and Economic Order* (Chicago: University of Chicago Press, 1948), 92–106.

8. Dominick Armentano, *Antitrust: The Case for Repeal* (Auburn, Alabama: Mises Institute, 1999), 55–56.

9. Ibid.

10. "The Right Stuff: America's Move to Mass Customization" (1998 Annual Report), Federal Reserve Bank of Dallas, https://www.dal lasfed.org/~/media/documents/fed/annual/1999/ar98.pdf.

11. Dominick Armentano, *Antitrust and Monopoly: Anatomy of a Policy Failure* (New York: Wiley, 1982), 40–42.

12. John S. McGee, "Predatory Price Cutting: The Standard Oil of New Jersey Case," *Journal of Law and Economics* 1 (October 1958): 137–69.

13. George Gilder, *The Spirit of Enterprise* (New York: Simon and Schuster, 1984), 155.

14. Ibid., 159.

15. William Shughart, *Antitrust Policy and Interest Group Politics* (Westport, Connecticut: Greenwood Press, 1990).

16. Armentano, *Antitrust and Monopoly.*

17. Ibid., 273.

Chapter 4: Bees, Keys, and Externalities

1. Arthur C. Pigou, *Wealth and Welfare* (Franklin Classics, 2018).

2. J. E. Meade, "External Economies and Diseconomies in a Competitive Situation," *Economics Journal* 52, (1952), 54.

3. Steven N. S. Cheung, "The Fable of the Bees: An Economic Investigation," *Journal of Law and Economics* 16 (1973), 13.

4. Ibid., 33.

5. Paul David, "Clio and the Economics of QWERTY," *American Economic Review* 75 (1985), 332. The "QWERTY" keyboard is named after the letters at the top left of most computer keyboards; the alternative "Dvorak" keyboard is named after the man who patented it.

6. Stan J. Liebowitz and Stephen E. Margolis, "The Fable of the Keys," *Journal of Law and Economics* 33 (1990), 10.

7. Ibid.

8. Ibid.

9. W. B. Arthur, "Positive Feedbacks in the Economy," *Scientific American* 262 (1990): 92–99.

10. James Griffiths, "The U.S. Is Still Using Floppy Discs to Run Its Nuclear Program," CNN, May 26, 2016, https://www.cnn.com/2016/05/26/us/pentagon-floppy-disks-nuclear/index.html.

11. Hana Schank and Sara Hudson, "The Outdated and Sorry State of Government Technology," The Lily, January 25, 2018, https://www.thelily.com/the-outdated-and-sorry-state-of-government-technology/.

12. Karl Zinmeister, "Japan's Industrial Policy Doesn't Work," *Policy Review* (Spring 1993): 28–35; Katsuroh Sakoh, "Japanese Economic Success: Industrial Policy or Free Market?," *Cato Journal* 4, no. 2 (Fall 1984): 521–48.

13. Robert Higgs, *Depression, War, and Cold War* (New York: Oxford University Press, 2006).

14. Ibid., 177.

15. Ibid., 180.

Chapter 5: Pollution: Is Capitalism the Cause— or the Cure?

1. Marshall Goldman, *The Spoils of Progress: Environmental Pollution in the Soviet Union* (Cambridge, Massachusetts: MIT Press, 1972), 66.

2. Ibid.

3. Peter Gumbel, "Soviet Concerns about Pollution Danger Are Allowed to Emerge from the Closet," *Wall Street Journal*, August 23, 1988.

4. Goldman, *The Spoils of Progress*, 225.

5. Ibid., 232.

6. Mike Femsilber, "Eastern Europe Fighting Worst Pollution in World," *Chattanooga Times*, January 17, 1990, 1.

7. Marlise Simons, "Rising Iron Curtain Exposes Haunting Veil of Polluted Air," *New York Times*, April 8, 1990.

8. Femsilber, "Eastern Europe Fighting Worst Pollution in World."

9. Garrett Hardin, "The Tragedy of the Commons," *Science* 162 (1968): 1243–48.

10. Murray Feshbach, *Ecocide in the USSR* (New York: Basic Books, 1993).

11. Richard Stroup, "Free-Market Environmentalism," Econlib, https://econlib.org/library/Enc/FreeMarketEnvironmentalism.html.

12. Morton J. Horwitz, *The Transformation of American Law, 1870–1960* (New York: Oxford University Press, 1993).

Chapter 6: The "Free-Rider" Fallacy

1. "Average Jail Time for Tax Evasion," Golding Lawyers, https://www.goldinglawyers.com/average-jail-time-for-tax-evasion-how-long-certified-tax-specialist/.

2. Kelly Erb, "Man Loses House after Failing to Pay $8.41 in Property Taxes," *Forbes*, December 6, 2019, https://www.forbes.com/sites/kellyphillipserb/2019/12/06/man-loses-home-after-failing-to-pay-841-in-property-taxes/?sh=7b514fa02a020.

3. Erik Nordman, *The Uncommon Knowledge of Elinor Ostrom* (Washington, D.C.: Island Press, 2021).

4. Donald Boudreaux, "The Private Provision of Public Goods," *The Freeman*, May 5, 2010, https://fee.org/articles/the-private-provision-of-public-goods/.

5. Ludwig von Mises, *Liberalism: The Classical Tradition* (Indianapolis: Liberty Fund, 2005).

6. Charles Murray, *Losing Ground: American Social Policy, 1950–1980* (New York: Basic Books, 2015).

7. Bruce Benson, *The Enterprise of Law: Justice Without the State* (Oakland, California: Independent Institute, 2011).

8. Alexander Hamilton, *Report on Manufactures*, in *Hamilton's Republic*, ed. Michael Lind (New York: Free Press, 1997), 31.

9. Carter Goodrich, *Government Promotion of American Canals and Railroads, 1800–1890* (Westport, Connecticut: Greenwood Press, 1960), 19.

10. Robert Rutland, *The Presidency of James Madison* (Lawrence, Kansas: University Press of Kansas, 1990), 205.

11. Andrew Jackson, "Farewell Address of Andrew Jackson," in Joseph L. Blau, *Social Theories of Jacksonian Democracy* (New York: Hafner, 1947), 305.

12. Daniel Klein, "The Voluntary Provision of Public Goods? The Turnpike Companies of Early America," *Economic Inquiry* (October 1990): 788–812.

13. Ibid., 797–98.

14. Ibid., 798.

15. William Herndon and Jesse Weik, *Life of Lincoln* (New York: Da Capo Press, 1983), 161.

16. Goodrich, *Government Promotion of Canals and Railroads*, 231.

17. Burton Folsom, *Entrepreneurs vs. the State: A New Look at the Rise of Big Business in America, 1840–1920* (Herndon, Virginia: Young America's Foundation, 1987), 28.

18. John Stuart Mill, *The Collected Works of John Stuart Mill*, vol. 3 (Indianapolis: Liberty Fund, 2006), 968.

19. Henry Sedgwick, *The Principles of Political Economy*, 306, available at https://laits.utexas.edu/poltheory/sidgwick/ppe/index.html.

20. Paul Samuelson, *Economics: An Introductory Analysis*, 6th ed. (New York: McGraw-Hill, 1964), 45.

21. Ronald Coase, "The Lighthouse in Economics," *Journal of Law and Economics* 17 (1974): 357–76.

22. Ibid., 361.

23. Ibid.

24. Ibid.

25. Ibid., 376.

Chapter 7: Un-Natural Monopolies

1. Harold Demsetz, *Efficiency, Competition, and Policy* (Cambridge, Massachusetts: Blackwell, 1989), 78.

2. Ibid.

3. F. A. Hayek, *The Road to Serfdom* (Chicago: University of Chicago Press, 1976), 197.

4. George T. Brown, *The Gas Light Company of Baltimore* (Baltimore: Johns Hopkins University Press, 1936).

5. Ibid., 75.

6. Horace M. Gray, "The Passing of the Public Utility Concept," *Journal of Land and Public Utility Economics* (February 1940), 9.

7. Ibid., 11.

8. Gregg Jarell, "The Demand for State Regulation of the Electric Utility Industry," *Journal of Law and Economics* (October 1978), 269.

9. Walter J. Primeaux, *Direct Electric Utility Competition: The Myth of Natural Monopoly* (New York: Praeger, 1986).

10. Thomas Hazlett, "Duopolistic Competition in Cable Television: Implications for Public Policy," *Yale Journal on Regulation* 7 (1990).

11. Adam Thierer, "Unnatural Monopoly: Critical Moments in the Development of the Bell System Monopoly," *Cato Journal* (Fall 1994): 267–85.

12. "Sherman Antitrust Act," Legal Information Institute, Cornell Law School, https://www.law.cornell.edu/wex/sherman_antitrust_act.

13. George Selgin, *Less than Zero: The Case for a Falling Price in a Growing Economy* (London: Institute for Economic Affairs, 1997).

14. Thomas DiLorenzo and Jack High, "Antitrust and Competition, Historically Contemplated," *Economic Inquiry* 26, no. 3 (July 1988): 423–35.

15. Richard T. Ely, *Monopolies and Trusts* (New York: MacMillan, 1990), 162.

16. DiLorenzo and High, "Antitrust and Competition."

17. George Stigler, "The Origin of the Sherman Act," *Journal of Legal Studies* 14, no. 1 (January 1985): 1–12.

18. Thomas DiLorenzo, "The Origins of Antitrust: An Interest-Group Perspective," *International Review of Law and Economics* 5, no. 1 (June 1985): 73–90.

19. Ibid.

20. Ibid.

21. "Tariff Extortion," *New York Times*, October 1, 1890, 2.

Chapter 8: Asymmetric (Backwards) Economics

1. George Akerlof, "The Market for Lemons: Quality Uncertainty and the Market Mechanism," *Quarterly Journal of Economics* 84 (1970): 488–500.

2. John Cassidy, "The Price Prophet," *New Yorker,* February 7, 2000, https://www.newyorker.com/magazine/2000/02/07/the-price-prophet.

3. Friedrich Hayek*, Individualism and Economic Order* (Chicago: University of Chicago Press, 1964), 80.

4. Ludwig von Mises, *Human Action: A Treatise on Economics* (Auburn, Alabama: Mises Institute, 1998).

5. Ibid., 325.

6. Gordon Tullock, Arthur Seldon, and Gordon Brady, *Government Failure: A Primer in Public Choice* (Washington, D.C.: Cato Institute, 2002).

7. "A–Z Index of U.S. Government Departments," usa.gov, https://www .usa.gov/federal-agencies.

8. "Ten Thousand Commandments," Competitive Enterprise Institute, https://cei.org/wp-content/uploads/2021/06/Ten_Thousand_Com mandments_2021.pdf.

9. "Congressional Re-election Rates," Open Secrets, https://www.open secrets.org/bigpicture/reelect.php.

Chapter 9: Creating Monopoly with Regulation

1. James Madison, *The Federalist* no. 51, available at the Library of Congress website, https://guides.loc.gov/federalist-papers/text-51 -60#s-lg-box-wrapper-25493427.

2. Milton Friedman and Rose Friedman, *Free to Choose: A Personal Statement* (New York: Harcourt Brace Jovanovich, 1980), 194.

3. Ibid., 195.

4. Ibid., 197.

5. Ibid., 198.

6. Ibid.

7. Ibid., 200.

8. "Vintage Photos Show How Glamorous the Golden Age of Air Travel Was," Kiwi Report, https://kiwireport.com/vintage-photos-show-how-glamorous-the-golden-age-of-air-travel-was-nttb/.

9. Alfred E. Kahn, "Airline Deregulation" Econlib, https://www.econlib.org/library/Enc1/AirlineDeregulation.html.

10. Ibid.

11. Friedman and Friedman, *Free to Choose*, 201.

12. Ibid.

13. Tyler Durden, "FDA Members Reviewing Pfizer Vaccine for Children Have Worked for Pfizer, Have Big Pfizer Connections," Zero Hedge, https://www.zerohedge.com/covid-19/fda-committee-members-reviewing-pfizer-vaccine-children-have-worked-pfizer-have-big-pfizer.

14. "Public Readiness and Emergency Preparedness Act," U.S. Department of Health and Human Services, https://www.phe.gov/Preparedness/legal/prepact/Pages/default.aspx.

15. Thomas Woods, *Meltdown* (Washington, D.C.: Regnery Publishing, 2009).

16. Walter E. Williams, *Race and Economics* (Stanford, California: Hoover Institution, 2011), 62.

17. Theresa Agovino, "How Much Is a NYC Taxi Medallion Worth These Days?," CBS News, April 14, 2017, https://www.cbsnews.com/news/how-much-is-a-nyc-taxi-medallion-worth-these-days/.

18. "Occupational Licensing Data Base," National Conference of State Legislatures, https://www.ncsl.org/research/labor-and-employment/occupational-licensing-statute-database.aspx.

19. Timothy Burger, "The Lobbying Game: Why the Revolving Door Won't Close," *Time*, February 6, 2006, https://web.archive.org/web/20060303114217/http://www.time.com/time/nation/article/0,8599,1160453,00.html.

20. "Washington in the Money," *Washingtonian*, November 2006, https://www.washingtonian.com/2006/11/01/november-2006-contents-in-the-money/.

Chapter 10: The Economics of Government Failure

1. William Shughart, "Public Choice," Econlib, https://www.econlib.org/library/Enc/PublicChoice.html.

2. James M. Buchanan and Gordon Tullock, *The Calculus of Consent* (Indianapolis: Liberty Fund, 1999).

3. "James M. Buchanan," Nobel Prize, http://www.nobelprize.org/prizes/economic-sciences/1986/buchanan/facts/.

4. James Madison, *The Federalist* no. 51, available at the Library of Congress website, https://guides.loc.gov/federalist-papers/text-51-60#s-lg-box-wrapper-25493427.

5. "Thomas Jefferson on Politics and Government," Family Guardian, https://famguardian.org/Subjects/Politics/ThomasJefferson/jeff1340.htm.

6. Mancur Olson, *The Rise and Decline of Nations* (New Haven: Yale University Press, 1984).

7. James Gwartney, Randall Holcombe, and Robert Lawson, "The Scope of Government and the Wealth of Nations," *Cato Journal* 18, no. 2 (Fall 1998): 163–90.

8. See Ludwig von Mises, *Bureaucracy* (Indianapolis: Liberty Fund, 2007); Gordon Tullock, *The Politics of Bureaucracy* (Washington, D.C.: Public Affairs Press, 1965); William Niskanen, *Bureaucracy and Representative Government* (London: Routledge, 2007).

9. Thomas Borcherding, *Budgets and Bureaucrats: The Sources of Government Growth* (Durham, North Carolina: Duke University Press, 1977).

10. William Meggison and Jeffrey Netter, "From State to Market: A Survey of Empirical Studies on Privatization," Organisation for Economic Co-operation and Development, August 31, 2000, https://www.oecd.org/daf/ca/corporategovernanceofstate-ownedenterprises/1929649.pdf.

11. Robert Higgs, *Crisis and Leviathan: Critical Episodes in the Growth of American Government* (New York: Oxford University Press, 1987).

12. Randolph Bourne, "War Is the Health of the State," Antiwar.com, January 1, 1918, https;//original.antiwar.com/rbourne/1918/01/01/war-is-the-health-of-the-state/.

13. Austin Peterson, "Government Preparing to Spread Washington Monument Syndrome," The Libertarian Republic, October 1, 2013, https://thelibertarianrepublic.com/government-preparing-spread-washington-monument-syndrome/.

Chapter 11: Who Creates Jobs? (And Who Destroys Them?)

1. Henry Hazlitt, *Economics in One Lesson* (New York: Laissez Faire Books, 2008).

2. U.S. Department of Commerce, *Historical Statistics of the United States* (Washington, D.C.: U.S. Government Printing Office, 1961), 73.

3. Richard Vedder and Lowell Gallaway, *Out of Work: Unemployment and Government in Twentieth-Century America* (New York: NYU Press, 1997).

4. "Historical Tables," Office of Management and Budget, The White House, https://www.whitehouse.gov/omb/budget/historical-tables/.

5. Robert Higgs, *Depression, War, and Cold War* (New York: Oxford University Press, 2006), 25.

6. Gary Walton and Hugh Rockoff, *History of the American Economy* (New York: Dryden Press, 1998), 408.

7. Michael Cox and Richard Alm, *Myths of Rich and Poor* (New York: Basic Books, 1999), 23.

8. Federal Reserve Bank of Dallas, *2000 Annual Report* (Dallas: Federal Reserve Bank of Dallas, 2000), 6.

9. For a list of several dozen such studies in peer-reviewed academic economics journals, see Walter E. Williams, *Race and Economics* (Stanford, California: Hoover Institution Press, 2011), 151–52.

10. David Card and Alan Krueger, "Minimum Wages and Employment: A Case Study of the Fast-Food Industry in New Jersey and Pennsylvania," *American Economic Review* 84, no. 4 (September 1994): 772–93.

11. David Neumark and William Wascher, "The Effects of New Jersey's Minimum Wage Increase on Fast-Food Employment: A Re-Evaluation Using Payroll Records" (Cambridge, Massachusetts: National Bureau of Economic Research, 1995).

12. "New Evidence on the Minimum Wage: The Crippling Flaws in the New Jersey Fast-Food Study," Employment Policies Institute, https://www.epionline.org/study_epi_njfast_04-1996.pdf.

13. "2021 Nobel Prize in Economics," Nobel Prize, https://www.nobelprize.org/prizes/economic-sciences/2021/press-release/.

14. Thomas Rustici, "A Public Choice View of the Minimum Wage," *Cato Journal* 5, no. 1 (Spring/Summer 1985): 103–120.

15. Rustici, "A Public Choice View of the Minimum Wage," 121.

16. Ibid., 124.

17. Ibid., 125.

18. Ibid.

19. Ibid., 127.

20. G. V. Doxey, *The Industrial Colour Bar in South Africa* (London: Oxford University Press, 1961), 156.

21. Morgan Reynolds, *Power and Privilege: Labor Unions in America* (New York: Universe Books, 1984), 53.

Chapter 12: The Fed: Government's Boom-and-Bust Machine

1. Paul Samuelson, *Economics* (New York: McGraw Hill, 2011), chapter 24.

2. Bob Woodward, *Maestro: Greenspan's Fed and the American Boom* (New York: Simon and Schuster, 2000).

3. Murray Rothbard, "The Myth of Fed Independence," Mises Institute, https://mises.org/daily/6365/.

4. Robert Weintraub, "Congressional Supervision of Monetary Policy," *Journal of Monetary Economics* 4, no. 2 (1978): 341–62.

5. Gerald O'Driscoll, "Debunking the Myths about Central Banks," *Wall Street Journal*, https://www.wsj.com/articles/SB10001424127 8873234686045782524439251554 34.

6. Murray Rothbard, *The Case Against the Fed* (Auburn, Alabama: Mises Institute, 2007).

7. David Stockman, *The Great Deformation: The Corruption of Capitalism in America* (New York: Public Affairs Press, 2013), xi.

8. Ibid., 45.

9. Ibid., 3.

10. Ibid., 7.

11. John R. Wilke, "Fed's Huge Empire, Set Up Years Ago, Is Costly and Inefficient," *Wall Street Journal*, September 12, 1996, 1.

12. Ibid.

13. George Selgin, William Lastrapes, and Lawrence H. White, "Has the Fed Been a Failure?" Cato Institute Working Paper, December 2010, https://www.cato.org/sites/cato.org/files/pubs/pdf/WorkingPaper-2.pdf.

14. Ibid., 3.

15. Ibid., 4.

16. Ibid., 7.

17. Ibid.

18. Ibid., 10.

19. Tom Woods, *Meltdown* (Washington, D.C.: Regnery Publishing, 2009), 94–95.

20. Ibid., 96.

21. Major L. Wilson, *The Presidency of Martin Van Buren* (Lawrence, Kansas: University Press of Kansas, 1984), 39.

22. Jeffrey Hummel, "Martin Van Buren: The American Gladstone," in John Denson, ed., *Reassessing the Presidency* (Auburn, Alabama: Mises Institute, 2001), 178.

23. Ibid.

24. Ibid., 188.

25. Ibid.

26. Murray Rothbard, "World War I as Fulfillment: Power and the Intellectuals," LewRockwell.com, https://www.lewrockwell.com/1970/01/murray-n-rothbard/power-and-the-intellectuals.

27. This account of Hoover's policies is adapted from Thomas DiLorenzo, *How Capitalism Saved America* (New York: Three Rivers Press, 2004), 160–75.

28. Woods, *Meltdown*, 26.

29. John Steele Gordon, "A Short History of Banking in the United States," *Wall Street Journal*, October 10, 2008, https://www.wsj.com/articles/SB122360636585322023.

30. Henry Kaufman, "How Libertarian Dogma Led the Fed Astray," *Financial Times*, https://www.ft.com/content/705574f2-3356-11de-8f1b-00144feabdcc0.

31. "The Federal Reserve: Purposes and Functions," Board of Governors of the Federal Reserve System, https://files.stlousfed.org/files/htdocs/econ/anderson/Purposes_and_Functions_9Apr2007.pdf?msclkid=51ee33ffa56611eca757aaa22619945f.

32. Lawrence H. White, "The Federal Reserve System's Influence on Research in Monetary Economics," *Econ Journal Watch* 2, no. 2 (August 2005): 325–54.

33. Ibid., 344.

34. Ibid.

35. F. A. Hayek, *Denationalization of Money* (London: Institute of Economic Affairs, 1977).

36. David Howden and Joseph T. Salerno, eds., *The Fed at One Hundred* (Springer, 2014), 168.

Chapter 13: The Root of All Evil

1. "Prohibition on Direct Taxation," Constitution Annotated, https://constitution.congress.gov/browse/essay/artl-S9-C4-1-1/ALDE_00001090/.

2. Harry Edwin Smith, *The United States Federal Income Tax History from 1861 to 1871* (New York: Houghton Mifflin Co., 1941), 66.

3. Ibid.

4. Arthur Ekirch Jr., "The Sixteenth Amendment: The Historical Background," *Cato Journal* (Spring 1981), 168.

5. Ibid., 177–78.

6. U.S. Bureau of the Census, *Historical Statistics of the United States* (Washington, D.C: U.S. Government Printing Office, 1960), 1095.

7. Edward Kaplan, "The Fordney-McCumber Tariff of 1922," EH.net, https://eh.net/encyclopedia/the-fordney-mccumber-tariff-of-1922/.

8. Frank Chodorov, *The Income Tax: Root of All Evil* (Greenwich, Connecticut: Devin-Adair, 1963).

9. Ibid., vi.

10. Ibid., 11.

11. "The Ten Planks of The Communist Manifesto," Conservative USA, https://www.conservativeusa.net/10planksofcommunism.htm.

12. Amity Shlaes, *The Greedy Hand: How Americans Are Being Taxed to Death* (New York: Random House, 1999).

13. Chodorov, *The Income Tax*, 48.

14. Ibid., 76.

15. Felix Morley, *Freedom and Federalism* (Chicago: H. Regnery Co., 1959), 103.

16. "Who Pays Income Taxes?," National Taxpayers Union Foundation, https://www.ntu.org/foundation/tax-page/who-pays-income-taxes.

17. "Federal Income Tax Brackets, 1980," Tax-Brackets.org, https:www.tax-brackets.org/federaltaxtable/1981.

18. "What Are the Seven Deadly Sins?," Bibleinfo, https://www.bibleinfo.com/en/questions/what-are-seven-deadly-sins.

19. Peter Sperry, "The Real Reagan Economic Record," Heritage Foundation, March 1, 2001, https://www.heritage.org/taxes/report/the-real-reagan-economic-record-responsible-and-successful-fiscal-policy.

20. Joseph T. Salerno, "What Ludwig von Mises Taught Gottfried Haberler and Paul Samuelson about Tax Loopholes," Mises Institute,

November 27, 2012, https://mises.org/wire/what-ludwig-von-mises
-taught-gottfried-haberler-and-paul-samuelson-about-tax-loopholes.

21. Doug Casey, "Slightly Up from Slavery," International Man, https://
    internationalman.com/articles/slightly-up-from-slavery/.

Chapter 14: "Trade Agreements" Are Not Free Trade

1. Thomas Paine, *Common Sense*, in *Complete Writings of Thomas Paine*, ed. Philip S. Foner (New York: Citadel Press, 1954), 20.

2. Ibid.

3. W. B. Allen, ed., *George Washington: A Collection* (Indianapolis: LibertyClassics, 1988), 525.

4. Ludwig von Mises, "The Economics of War," in *Human Action* (Auburn, Alabama: Mises Institute, 1999), chapter 34.

5. Llewellyen Rockwell, "Maybe We Should Call It SHAFTA," *Los Angeles Times*, October 19, 1992, https://www.latimes.com/archives/la-xpm-1992-10-19-me-371-story.html.

6. Ibid.

7. "Why Did Whimpy Always Say 'I'll Gladly Pay You Tuesday for a Hamburger Today' on the Cartoon Popeye?," Quora, https://www.quora.com/Why-did-Wimpy-always-say-Ill-gladly-pay-you-Tuesday-on-the-cartoon-Popeye.

8. Rockwell, "Maybe We Should Call it SHAFTA."

9. Quoted in James Sheehan, *Two Years After NAFTA* (Washington, D.C.: Competitive Enterprise Institute, 1996), 4.

10. Ibid., 19.

Chapter 15: Socialism (Or How to Destroy an Economy, Impoverish People, and Deprive Them of Their Freedoms)

1. Robert Heilbroner, "The Triumph of Capitalism," *New Yorker*, January 16, 1989.

2. Ludwig von Mises, *Socialism: An Economic and Sociological Analysis* (Auburn, Alabama: Mises Institute, 2009).

3. F. A. Hayek, *The Road to Serfdom* (Chicago: University of Chicago Press, 1976).

4. Mises, *Socialism*, 414.

5. Thomas DiLorenzo, "The Myth of Successful Scandinavian Socialism," in *The Problem with Socialism* (Washington, D.C. Regnery, 2016), 77–84.

6. Rafael Acevedo, "How Socialism Ruined Venezuela," Mises Institute, https://mises.org/library/how-socialism-ruined-venezuela.

7. Mises, *Socialism*, 417.

8. Yaron Steinbach, "Black Lives Matter Co-Founder Describes Herself as 'Trained Marxist,'" *New York Post*, June 25, 2020, https://nypost.com/2020/06/25/blm-co-founder-describes-herself-as-trained-marxist/.

9. Mises, *Socialism*, 423.

10. Murray N. Rothbard, "The End of Socialism and the Calculation Debate Revisited," Mises Institute, July 31, 2021, https://mises.org/library/end-socialism-and-calculation-debate-revisited.

11. F. A. Hayek, *The Fatal Conceit: Errors of Socialism* (Chicago: University of Chicago Press, 1991).

12. Murray N. Rothbard, "Freedom, Inequality, Primitivism, and the Division of Labor," in Murray N. Rothbard, *The Logic of Action II:*

Applications and Criticism from the Austrian School (Chatham, UK: Edward Elgar, 1997), 27.

13. H. L. Mencken, *A Mencken Chrestomathy* (New York: Alfred A. Knopf, 1949), 145..

14. Kurt Vonnegut Jr., "Harrison Bergeron," in *Welcome to the Monkey House* (New York: Dell, 1970), 7.5.

15. Rothbard, "Freedom, Inequality, Primitivism, and the Division of Labor," 16.

16. Ibid., 79.

17. Bruce Caldwell, ed., *The Road to Serfdom: Text and Documents: The Definitive Edition* (Chicago: University of Chicago Press, 2007), 246.

18. Ibid.

19. Hayek, *The Road to Serfdom*, 56.

20. Ibid., 92.

21. Ibid., 135.

22. Ibid., 138.

23. Ibid., 139.

24. Ibid., 160.

25. Ibid., 163.

26. John C. Goodman, Gerald Musgrave, and Devon M. Herrick, *Lives at Risk: Single-Payer National Health Insurance Around the World* (Lanham, Maryland: Roman and Littlefield, 2004), 19.

27. Ibid., 18.

28. Ibid., 21.

29. Thomas J. DiLorenzo, *The Problem with Socialism* (Washington, D.C.: Regnery, 2016), 98.

30. Ibid., 100.

31. Ibid.

32. Yuri Maltsev, "What Soviet Medicine Teaches Us," Mises Institute, June 22, 2012, http://mises.org/library/what-soviet-medicine-teaches-us.

33. Ibid.

34. Ibid. Professor Maltsev once took a group of college students to Cuba for a "study abroad" trip and concluded that the only way for an average person to get good medical care there was, in his words, to "swim to Miami."

Epilogue

1. Ludwig von Mises, *Human Action: A Treatise* (Auburn, Alabama: Mises Institute, 1968), 868.

2. Ibid.

3. Ibid.

4. Ibid., 871.

5. Ibid.

6. Ibid.

7. Ibid., 874.

8. Ibid., 875.

Index